THE INTEGRITY
OF
ANGLICANISM

THE INTEGRITY

OF

ANGLICANISM

STEPHEN W. SYKES

A Crossroad Book
THE SEABURY PRESS / NEW YORK

1978
The Seabury Press
815 Second Avenue
New York, N.Y. 10017

Printed in the United States of America

Library of Congress Cataloging in Publication Data
Sykes, Stephen.   The integrity of Anglicanism.
"A Crossroad book."
Includes bibliographical references and index.
1. Anglican Communion—Doctrinal and controversial works.
2. Theology, Anglican.   I. Title.
BX5005.S94   230'.3   78-19034   ISBN 0-8164-0405-4

There's this to be said for the Church [of England], a man can belong to the Church and bide in his cheerful old inn, and never trouble or worry his mind about doctrines at all.

Coggan, in Thomas Hardy's
Far from the Madding Crowd

CONTENTS

ANGLICANS are not supposed to know about, or to be interested in, systematic theology. But it seems to me that the most helpful prefatory remark I can make is that the internal divisions within Anglicanism, the subject of this book, can be best understood with the help of a critical grasp of systematic theology. Indeed the book is written on the basis of the conviction that systematic theology cannot safely be neglected, not even by Anglicans; and that, within systematics, it is the doctrine of the church which Anglicans especially need to recognise as occupying a fundamental place.

By 'systematic theology' I mean that constructive discipline which presents the substance of the Christian faith with a claim on the minds of men. In this sense I am content to use the terms 'systematic theology' and 'doctrinal theology' interchangeably, although I realise that a more precise use of terms would reserve 'systematics' for the presentation of Christian theology in the context of a philosophically systematic understanding of the world.

Anglicans are never far from being painfully aware of their internal divisions, and at present these are vividly before the public. But Anglican apologists have not always seen that their attempts to explain how all the various viewpoints coexist in one communion raise extremely far-reaching issues about the nature of the church. By 'the church' I mean not just the Anglican church, but the universal Church of Christ in which the Anglican church claims to participate. Anglicans have no permission to regard their own communion as somehow immune from the critical questions to which any systematic doctrine of the church must give rise. In the kingdom of God there are no quiet meadows where tired old churches can be put out to grass.

So the question is, how are Anglicans to understand their communion? Not, certainly, as though they believed it to be an end in itself. I would not wish anyone's loyalty to Anglicanism to be more than strictly penultimate. But neither, on the other hand, should Anglicans come to believe that it scarcely matters if their communion flutters to and fro, tolerantly receptive to every passing opinion. Spiritually, that would be disastrous;

theologically, it would be irresponsible. And it is one of my chief aims to show how and why the discipline of systematic theology, applied to the position which the Anglican church actually occupies, can contribute to a deeper self-understanding, and to a more rigorous self-criticism.

I am far from thinking, however, that the rectifying of this weakness would be a cure for the vast array of ailments attributed to contemporary Anglicanism. Good systematic theology will not, of itself, fill pews, produce saints, or open purses. Systematic theology is an intellectual discipline and only part of the Christian's offering of himself to God. As such it ought to be accorded no more, but also no less, than the attention which it deserves. As an intellectual discipline, if any systematic theology can be successfully accused of being 'merely academic' in the sense of having no point of contact with human lives, then it is simply bad systematic theology. Thinking the subject through properly is the only known antidote.

My thanks to Professor Howard Root of the University of Southampton for permission to print a letter published in *The Times*; to Margaret Hutchison, who worked with me on the question of membership of the church; to Michael Perry, Archdeacon of Durham, who commented acutely on the original typescript; and, especially to Paul Wignall, Precentor of Durham Cathedral, who has discussed most of these issues with me, and who has added an independent, but complementary essay on 'Patterns in Theology', printed at the end of the book.

A QUESTION OF INTEGRITY

THE term integrity has evidently two major meanings. In the first place it can be used to speak of the completeness of some particular object or institution. In this sense one can speak of a building standing 'in its integrity' or 'in its entirety', and of the 'integrity of the law', meaning its unimpaired state. In these cases 'integrity' indicates the capacity to recognise the whole identity of the object or institution, as something which is not deficient or impaired. In the second place, however, there is the more familiar moral connotation to the term, especially when applied to the character of an individual. The 'integrity' of a man is his uprightness, honesty or sincerity; of an institution or group of men their acting according to high standards of moral principle. The title of this book, 'The Integrity of Anglicanism', is intended to draw meaning from both these senses. The first sense of the term accounts for all the particular topics which are raised in the course of these chapters; and the second, as I shall try to explain at the end of this introduction, accounts for the note of concern in the way in which these topics are written about.

First, then, the question is whether or not Anglicanism has a coherent identity: that is, whether it constitutes something which is recognisable. If Anglicanism has no such identity, then one ought not to use the word. It can be dropped from the vocabulary as an ultimately misleading word, which, though once upon a time people thought was useful, now turns out to be systematically incoherent. It would not merely be the term 'Anglicanism' of which we would have to dispose; the word 'Anglican' could hardly survive, especially in that comforting and ambiguous form, 'the Anglican church'. For to inquire into the identity of Anglicanism is to ask whether there is any internal rationale binding Anglicans together as 'church'.

Even as one poses the question thus one can hear a chorus of doubts about the form of the inquiry. Questions as to the nature of X, where X is something abstract like courage or honour or duty, make the mistake of turning X into something like a substance, whose nature can be made plain by suitable analysis. In all such cases there is a prior question to be asked, namely whether X is something about which an inquiry as to its nature can appropriately be mounted. What, then, about a term like 'Anglicanism'? Is this not similarly abstract? Should we not first ask whether Anglicanism is some one thing or entity before plunging into an inquiry as to its identity.

Happily one can be quite brief with these doubts. Anglicanism is not something abstract like courage, but is the quality of being Anglican which belongs to an actually existent series of bodies in communion with, and recognising the leadership of, the see of Canterbury. There is no reason why the nature of Anglicanism should be something simple or easily definable; it could easily consist in something complex and diffuse. Thus it is very appropriate to warn ourselves at the outset of the inquiry against the temptation to oversimplify. Nonetheless, being an Anglican means something, in as much as one has no particular difficulty in distinguishing being an Anglican from being a Plymouth Brother or a Seventh Day Adventist. And what that something is, is the point of this inquiry.

The theoretical question as to the status of an inquiry into the identity of Anglicanism can thus be laid on one side because of quite practical and factual considerations. There exist texts in which the churches of the Anglican communion lay out what is involved in membership of the church, or what is involved in admission to its ordained ministry. It is quite clear that one can quite sensibly ask what is the content of these texts, and what is the justification for the conditions laid down. The answers to these questions supply much of the information needed for the inquiry into the identity of Anglicanism. The second, similarly practical, consideration is the long history of attempts to expound the inner rationale of Anglicanism. The mere existence of this literature would justify an inquiry into the arguments frequently employed in them, and a considerable amount of the substance of this book consists in such an examination.

There is, however, a serious theological doubt about the appropriateness of assuming that Anglicanism constitutes a complete or self-sufficient identity. This doubt is given expression by one who must be reckoned as among the most profound interpreters of Anglicanism in this century, in words which are justly famous. Michael Ramsey writes:

'While the Anglican church is vindicated by its place in history,
with a strikingly balanced witness to Gospel and Church and
sound learning, its greater vindication lies in its pointing
through its own history to something of which it is a fragment.
Its credentials are its incompleteness, with the tension and the
travail in its soul. It is clumsy and untidy, it baffles neatness
and logic. For it is sent not to commend itself as 'the best
type of Christianity', but by its very brokenness to point to
the universal Church wherein all have died.'[1]

In comment on this portrait of Anglicanism I would offer
the following remark at this stage, referring the reader to later
chapters of the book for a fuller discussion. Ramsey regards the
Anglican church at once as broken or incomplete, and also as a
sign capable of pointing to that which is greater than it. But
precisely as a sign it must possess sufficient coherent identity to
be recognisable as such. I am in profound agreement with
Ramsey in his theological interpretation of Anglicanism as a
communion uniquely committed to labour for a greater unity,
and conscious of its own incompleteness as a church. But
incompleteness is something other than incoherence; and my
concern here is to establish whether or not the Anglican
Communion has strayed from the one to the other — to inquire,
in other words, whether it can sensibly be regarded as a sign of
anything Christianly significant whatsoever.

One is encouraged, the moment one turns to some of the
most perceptive writers dealing with these questions, to discover
doubts expressed on precisely this score. In 1929, for example,
A. E. J. Rawlinson pertinently asked:

'Does the Church of England possess genuine internal cohesion
and unity? Was not the Bishop of Zanzibar [Frank Weston]
in the right when he described it as having 'an exceedingly
chaotic system of truth'? To what is the Anglican Church
really committed in matters of doctrine, and for what does it
stand? Has it an intelligible *raison d'être* as a specific variant of
the Christian tradition in the midst of a Christendom which
more and more seeks after unity?'[2]

Or again, in a letter written in 1947 to Dean Selwyn of Win-
chester, Bishop Hensley Henson drew attention to the publication of two works by Anglican bishops, one, K. E. Kirk's
The Apostolic Ministry, containing an argument affirming the
necessity of episcopacy to the essential being of the church, the
other, Bishop Barnes' *Rise of Christianity*, in Henson's words,
'a highly effective attack on the Christian tradition'. He
continued:

> 'The first is in my judgement definitely, in tone, in type, temper and tendency not Anglican but Roman, and the last is not even, in any tolerable sense, Christian. Yet the authors are Bishops, holding office as such in the Church of England. How long can that kind of comprehension be maintained, or rightly defended? I do not think it possible that any Church can long cohere when such radical divergence on essentials is acquiesced in.'[3]

The question is also faced with commendable directness by one of the committees reporting to the 1948 Lambeth conference.

> 'The question is asked, 'Is Anglicanism based on a sufficiently coherent form of authority to form the nucleus of a world-wide fellowship of Churches, or does its comprehensiveness conceal internal divisions which may cause its disruption?'[4]

The 'integrity of Anglicanism' means, then, in the first instance, its coherent identity; and as a whole the sections of this book reflect the numerous considerations to which an inquiry into its identity gives rise. In the first place we have to examine the deployment of the idea of the comprehensiveness of the Anglican communion, since that idea is repeatedly used by both official and unofficial apologists for Anglicanism. The most recent official document to refer to the comprehensiveness of the Anglican communion is a report to the Lambeth conference of 1968. The first chapter of the book is, accordingly, devoted to an analysis of the rather diverse elements which have contributed to the popularity of the idea, and to an account of the contemporary crisis into which it has now fallen. The next chapter pursues the major reason for the crisis, which is, clearly enough, the theological activities of those whose writings now-adays cause the same kind of offence as that given by Barnes' *Rise of Christianity*. Although what these theologians say is not identical with what the Anglican modernists of the first half of the twentieth century were saying, the resemblances are neither slight nor incidental. Their theology may be spoken of as liberal in as much as it is highly critical of the beliefs of many in the Church of England, who think of themselves as close to orthodox Anglican traditions, whether Evangelical or Anglo-Catholic; and to this extent they have a right to be regarded as standing in the succession of a long, but diverse tradition of liberal theology in the Anglican communion. The question to be asked, however, is whether or not mistakes have been made in the identification of this tradition and in the terms on which it has been thought possible to include it in the ample 'comprehensiveness' of the Anglican church.

The major, and often recognised, problem which this tradition poses, is whether there are or could be any limits to the toleration extended to liberals within the Anglican church. In this connection the following chapter investigates the significance of liturgy and canon law, where, if anywhere, the possibility of the enforcement of orthodoxy (or of 'orthopraxy', if liturgy is regarded as an activity) arises for Anglicans. No matter whether the inquiry into the belief of an Anglican official is framed in widely tolerant terms, the promise which is extracted limiting him or her to the use of prescribed forms of public worship is close and binding. Even so, within this framework, there is still a considerable freedom; and both the framework and the freedom need theological interpretation, providing the Anglican church with considerable material for making clear its standpoint.

Three further questions suggest themselves at this point, and are specifically raised for discussion in the following chapters. Is there an Anglican theology, a proposal which many have denied? Is there an Anglican method in theology, which some have affirmed while denying that there is an Anglican theology? And what in any case is the present state of Anglican study of the doctrine of the church, and why is there so little deliberate cultivation of doctrinal or systematic theology? These three questions arise if it is agreed that there is a way of articulating the Anglican standpoint. The discipline in which the articulation of a Roman Catholic or an Orthodox standpoint would occur would be called dogmatic theology, which would be written on the basis of sources which those communions regard as authoritative. Thus in the final chapter, I shall attempt to face directly the question which lies behind the whole Anglican hesitancy about its self-understanding, namely the question of authority in Anglicanism.

But there is also, as I have mentioned, a second meaning to the term 'integrity', which is its reference to a state of moral soundness. I would myself be less than honest if I did not admit that part of my concern for contemporary Anglicanism is precisely on this score. To put it bluntly, there is something corrupt about an institution which presumes to mould the Christian allegiance of its millions of members and officially states that it bears testimony to the gospel of Christ, but which is unwilling or unable to face the issues of belief which are immediately apparent to any informed Christian. I have no doubt that many will see in these statements an appeal for what was once, and still may be, called 'definite teaching' (that is, dogmatic views on all the subjects which have, in the course of time, been matters of Christian theological discussion). But that is not my intended meaning. A Christian church, which is aware of a wide variety of diverse theological positions and which deliberately decides not to adopt one or other of them, but rather to tolerate diversity, has still to offer a definite reason for doing so and to justify that reason in the face of objection. If a church both enforces the use of a liturgy which is thoroughly stamped by a particular doctrinal inheritance, and also permits wide latitude in the professed belief of its officers, then, again, there ought to be a thorough analysis and explanation of that dual position. And my complaint against the Church of England, in particular, is that its attempts to do so hitherto have been muddled and inadequate, partly by reason of the continued use of an apologetic which patently no longer meets the situation (if it ever did) and partly because of deeply rooted failures in its programme of theological education.

A recent monograph on the Victorian debates about the ethics of assenting to the Thirty Nine Articles and the creeds concludes with some remarks about the Church of England (it was written, it should be noted, before the new Declaration and Oath of Assent, see page 36):

> 'With all its limitations exposed and with due modifications made, it would be well if that ethical concern over belief which so exercised the late Victorians would once again be recognised as a moral responsibility. At least Leslie Stephen and his friends believed that no society could long survive the erosion of such a moral ideal — and in this they were surely right.'[5]

This 'moral ideal' concerns not merely individuals, in their struggle to relate the beliefs which they profess in their churches to those of their deepest convictions. It concerns also whole Christian communities, and especially the leaders of these communities, in their struggle to articulate how their church participates in the Universal Church of Christ, and seeks to bring in his kingdom. Toleration of diversity itself needs to be justified theologically if it is to be able to claim any kind of integrity. There is a point at which a natural desire to avoid a fuss shades off into an unwillingness to seek for any clarity; and another point at which a serious, but corrigible state of muddle shades off into a loss of integrity. It may be that the antidote to such a decline is to be resolutely aware from the first of the moral responsibility inherent in the very nature of Christian belief, even at the cost of conflict and the temptation to dramatize what is in any way a matter for the striking of poses.

Conflict, it must be admitted, seems almost to have been a way of life for our Victorian forefathers; and it was at least in part to mitigate the sharpness of the exchanges between Anglicans of different persuasions in the nineteenth century, that the theory of comprehensiveness of the Anglican communion was raised to a key position in Anglican apologetic. To its analysis and criticism, therefore, we must first turn.

FOOTNOTES

1. A. M. Ramsey, *The Gospel and the Catholic Church* (London, 1936), p. 220
2. *The Church of England and the Church of Christ* (London, 1930), pp. viii-ix
3. E. F. Braley (ed), *Letters of Herbert Hensley Henson* (London, 1951), p. 204
4. *The Lambeth Conference 1948* (London, 1948), Part II, p. 84
5. James C. Livingston, *The Ethics of Belief, An Essay on the Victorian Religious Conscience* (Tallahassee, Florida, 1974), p. 59

Chapter 1

THE CRISIS OF ANGLICAN
COMPREHENSIVENESS
(*Indecisiveness* ?)

COMPREHENSIVENESS in the context of the understanding of a church means simply that that church contains in itself many elements regarded as mutually exclusive in other communions. All churches are comprehensive in certain other respects, for example, in their inclusion of members of both sexes and of all ages. But one would only speak of the 'comprehensiveness of the Anglican communion' if one had in mind some implicit contrast between the Anglican communion and other bodies. So comprehensiveness is most often and most naturally associated with the inclusion of protestant and catholic elements (and, sometimes, as we shall see of other elements as well) in the one fellowship.

It is also the case that the Anglican communion is not literally all-embracing. As a matter of fact it was unable to include many of those protestants of the sixteenth or seventeenth centuries who felt that the Anglican reformation had been incompletely faithful to the scriptures. It still does not contain those who reject episcopacy as a system of church government, nor those who insist on receiving the eucharistic sacrament only from priests in communion with the Pope. If it fails to comprehend those on the one side, who, hold dogmas contrary to its own so does it also fail to comprehend those, on the other side, who see no reason to hold any beliefs at all. Not even the Church of England is as tolerantly comprehensive as an open debating society, which would stand solely for the open discussion of any view whatsoever.

Comprehensiveness is, therefore, *per se*, a radically unclear notion, requiring qualification to give it precision; and it is for this reason that when it is used in Anglican apologetic it has to be used in contexts which make clear both what is comprehended and what is still excluded. There is an understandable sensitivity to the suggestion that in Anglicanism anything goes. Even those who like to champion doctrinal freedom on matters which the tradition of Christian orthodoxy has for centuries considered unchallengeable within the bounds of the Christian communion — doctrinal matters like the doctrines of the Trinity or of the Incarnation — are less keen on the toleration of doctrines with clear practical consequences, like the essential masculinity of the priesthood or the racial doctrines of certain elements of the Dutch Reformed Church of South Africa. Indeed the question is sometimes raised by Anglican apologists whether comprehensiveness has anything at all to do with toleration.

What then is claimed for Anglican comprehensiveness? I am going to take my answer to this question from the pages of the 1968 Lambeth Conference report. Then I propose to subject the statement found there to a brief analysis, and finally to illustrate the historical origins of the elements of the statement; from all of which it will emerge that there are some important problems awaiting clarification.

The comprehensiveness of the Anglican Communion was spoken of in one of the 1968 Lambeth Conference Reports as follows:

> 'Comprehensiveness demands agreement on fundamentals, while tolerating disagreement on matters in which Christians may differ without feeling the necessity of breaking communion. In the mind of an Anglican, comprehensiveness is not compromise. Nor is it to bargain one truth for another. It is not a sophisticated word for syncretism. Rather it implies that the apprehension of truth is a growing thing: we only gradually succeed in 'knowing the truth'.'

It is perhaps worth pausing to note that element of sensitivity towards criticism of comprehensiveness from outside Anglicanism. The section quoted is from a comment on discussions with Orthodox churches, who themselves claim comprehensiveness, albeit in a different sense, and with whom there has been a continuing exchange of views on this topic.[1]

Two points are made in reply to the supposed charges that comprehensiveness involves compromise and syncretism. The first, that there must be agreement on fundamentals, is, as we shall see, a very long-standing Anglican position. The second, that the apprehension of 'truth' is a developing matter, is a consideration of the utmost generality, applied to the comprehensiveness of Anglicanism in the following way:

> 'It has been the tradition of Anglicanism to contain within one body both Protestant and Catholic elements. But there is a continuing search for the whole truth in which these elements

will find complete reconciliation. Comprehensiveness implies a
willingness to allow liberty of interpretation, with a certain
slowness in arresting or restraining exploratory thinking.'[2]

Analysis of this statement suggests that it contains three
elements. (First) and without any ambiguity, there is the affirmation of a comprehensiveness limited and qualified by agreement
on fundamentals. This qualification establishes the fact that
excluded from the comprehensiveness of Anglicanism are views
which contradict the fundamentals and views which assert as
fundamental matters which Anglicans hold to be non-funda-
mental. (Secondly,) there is the assertion that Anglicanism
contains within itself both protestant and catholic elements,
which will, in the continuing search for the whole truth, one
day be completely reconciled. The implication of this affirmation is that at the present moment these elements are unrecon-
ciled. Hence, one can speak of their complementarity, meaning
that both are necessary to the whole truth despite the fact that
they appear contradictory. And, (thirdly,) there appears the view
that there is a development in apprehension of the truth. In the
statement as quoted this point is closely linked to the second,
but it is, in fact, a separate proposal. Comprehensiveness is said
to imply 'a willingness to allow liberty of interpretation', and it
is directly asserted that not merely did the circumstances of the
Anglican reformation present the Anglican communion with
apparently divergent elements, but the 'exploratory thinking'
of the present and future may do so likewise. 'We believe',
the Report continues, 'that in leading us into all the truth the
Holy Spirit may have some surprises in store for us in the future
as he has had in the past' (p. 141). This happy and characteristic
piece of modern Anglican euphoria has a complex background,
and its combination with the second point shows a rather confused weaving together of strands which it will be necessary to
disentangle. But what it is sufficient to remark on here is simply
the fact that the 'doctrine of new truth' (as it may be called) is
independent of the principle of complementarity. Although the
resolution of complementarity may be said to involve new truth,
the possibility of new truth emerging out of exploratory thinking
does not require a prior state of complementary truths held in
tension. These two ideas have different backgrounds, as we shall
see, and are simply woven together at this point in order to
introduce a much broader notion of comprehensiveness than is

contained in the earlier parts of the statement. It will be the particular task of this and the next chapter to elucidate the difficulties contained in this all too briefly introduced breadth, but first some background to all the elements of the statement must be offered.

We ask, then, how, historically speaking, these three elements have arisen in the Anglican communion. The answers can be given in no more than the broadest of strokes, but since the outlines are reasonably well known it will perhaps be sufficient merely to refer readers to the literature which is readily available.

1. First, we must comment on the tradition of speaking about agreement on fundamentals. The distinction between the fundamental articles of the Christain faith and matters which are merely accessory to it is clearly drawn by Hooker. Near the opening of his third book on the *Laws of Ecclesiastical Polity* (1594) he speaks of the unity of the visible church as grounded in the outward profession of 'the essence of Christianity' (the first occurrence of this term in English known to me), which profession is necessary in every Christian man. Furthermore he makes explicitly clear that by the 'essence of Christianity' he means the articles of Christian belief given as the *regula fidei* in the works of Irenaeus and Tertullian. These fundamentals are, in effect, the propositions which go to make up the Nicene and Apostles' creeds minus some of the late attempts at precision deriving from the circumstances of the Arian controversy. They constitute, Hooker asserts, the faith which Jesus taught and which has characterised the visible church from that day to this. They are present in the Roman church, and although quite wrongly Rome has added to this primitive faith much which is secondary or corrupt nonetheless it has not denied the fundamentals and so stands as part of the visible church. This particular understanding of the significance of fundamental articles is constantly repeated by Anglican writers of the late sixteenth and early seventeenth centuries. So important is this doctrine that Chillingworth, one of the major Anglican apologists of the seventeenth century affirmed that for the Church to be the church implied that it must be *infallible* in fundamentals.[3] Moreover it is to this tradition that Newman appeals in his Anglican lectures on the *Prophetical Office of the Church* (1837). Here we find him also referring to Tertullian and Irenaeus, citing Bishop William van Mildert (1765-1836) on the glories of this

unvaried and invariable tradition, and contrasting the fixity of the essentials of Anglicanism so understood with the regrettable tendency of the Roman creed to grow.

The contemporary power and attractiveness of this tradition is amply demonstrated by a letter of Professor H. E. Root to *The Times*, published on 1 June 1977 (and printed in full in the Appendix). Root writes as a participator in the Anglican-Roman Catholic commission which has met since 1970 to discuss central questions dividing Anglicans from Roman Catholics in the sphere of ecclesiology, namely, the ministry, the sacraments and the question of authority in the church. Commenting on correspondence arising from the charge of vagueness or ambiguity in modern Anglican teaching on the sacraments, Root explicitly used the distinction between fundamentals and the (secondary) theological interpretation of fundamentals as a way of establishing limits to diversity. Here, however, it is noticeable that the fundamentals are not said to be the articles of the Nicene or Apostles' creeds; nor even to consist in any particular set of propositions. The fundamental rock of agreement is, nonetheless, so he claimed, 'the 'Nicene faith', that Christ was the incarnate Word of God'. If many Anglicans or Roman Catholics could not accept this, or were hesitant about it, there would, he claimed, be little point in searching for unity in other matters which stemmed from the fundamentals.

I do not propose at this juncture to offer a discussion of this long tradition of theological distinction between fundamentals and non-fundamentals as a means of establishing limits to the comprehensiveness claimed for the Anglican communion. But it will be obvious enough that in the form in which it is affirmed by Hooker, Chillingworth, van Mildert and Newman this tradition would not escape criticism at the hands of modern theologians. With what justice, it would be asked, can it be said that the faith taught by Christ is identical with that found in the *regula fidei* of the second century, or in the orthodox creeds of the fourth century? And there would be many who would question whether it is in any way conceivable that the faith of those early centuries could be understood and believed by modern man in the precise way in which it was understood and believed by Christians of those times. Even if the identical words were used, it would certainly be the case that their meanings would have changed. There would be many who would have considerable sympathy for some of the reasons which led Newman to abandon his Anglican belief in the fixity of the essentials of the creed for his more sophisticated notions of continuity in development. At the very least one must say that the growth of greater sensitivity towards the linkage of religious and secular thought, and awareness of the different mental horizons of men of earlier centuries, renders the confidence of a Hooker, of a Chillingworth or of a van Mildert problematical.

Moreover it is no doubt for this reason, among others, that Root does not identify the fundamentals with certain articles of the creed, but with 'the Nicene faith'. For in this way of expressing the fundamentals there need be no claim that one particular set of statements with fixed and unalterable meanings embodies that faith. Indeed that one faith might be held to be inexpressible in any one fully complete and unalterable form. Nonetheless, the whole point of referring to the Nicene faith (rather than the faith of some of the heterodox councils of the fourth century) would be to affirm that at Nicaea something was stated in verbal form about God's self-revelation which is paradigmatic for any future expression of a faith which is Christian. By a paradigm one means a standard instance of what is under consideration, that is, the verbal expression of the content of Christian belief. If it is not the case that the propositions of the creed of the Council of Nicaea are the fixed and unalterable truths of Christianity nonetheless it is the case, according to this way of thinking, that the faith which came to expression in what was said by the orthodox fathers at Nicaea constitutes the fundamentals of any form of Christianity with a claim to be Christian. Thus it follows that the propositional form of the 'Nicene faith' is, in this more indirect sense, paradigmatic; and this too is a position which at least some Anglican theologians would feel constrained to deny, and for the same reasons as were brought against the earlier, less sophisticated version of the theory.

Now whether or not this opposition to the idea of fundamentals is significant in Anglicanism, or is a piece of tolerable academic eccentricity, is something we shall have to discuss at a later stage. For the moment it is sufficient to observe that there is a distinction between saying, as Hooker and many others do, that belief in the fundamental articles is necessary to salvation, and saying, as Newman did, that the proclamation of the fundamental articles is necessary for the integrity of the church. A church may well have a certain public statement of its faith and be largely tolerant of internal dissent. This seems to be Professor Root's position. If *many* Anglicans or Roman Catholics came to doubt the Nicene faith then there would be no point in speaking of it in any real sense as constituting the fundamentals. If *certain* Anglicans state their doubt that 'Nicene faith' is paradigmatic in the way it has repeatedly been said to be in public statements, this does not *ipso facto* alter the church's public stance; and whether or not disciplinary action is taken against the doubters is more a question of how it understands the authority of its bishops and councils than a question of the breadth of its doctrinal tolerance. To this, as I have already noted, we shall have to return. Perhaps sufficient has been said to demonstrate both the historical roots of the question and its controversial character in modern discussion.

2. The second historical comment which is required is a reference to the concept of the *Via Media*. Modern Anglicans show themselves somewhat touchy when it is suggested that Anglicanism set itself to a middle course by means of a deliberate avoidance of extremes.[4] But there can be no doubt that the conscious self-portraiture of a church pursuing a path of conservative reformation has made a deep impact on Anglican thinking. Speaking of the reform of the liturgy, the Preface to the 1662 Book of Common Prayer opens with the classic statement:

> 'It hath been the wisdom of the Church of England, ever since the first compiling of her Publick Liturgy; to keep the mean between two extremes, of too much stiffness in refusing, and of too much easiness in admitting any variation from it.'

George Herbert's British Church, 'neither too mean, nor yet too gay' and Bishop Patrick's 'virtuous mediocrity . . . between the meretricious gaudiness of the Church of Rome and the squalid sluttery of fanatic conventicles' proclaim a self-understanding distinct from, by being midway between, the polity of either one or the other. The very convenience of the mediational self-designation, however, is the source of some theological embarrassment. Could it be that the *Via Media* is but an unhappy compromise, born of practical or even political motivation? Are there good, indeed are there any, theological grounds for this position, or is it the result of a poverty of thought and of a sheer reluctance to attempt to come to grips with intractably difficult theological material?

There can be no historical doubt that it was the intention of the architects of the Elizabethan settlement to provide a context in which men of widely differing theological conviction could coexist. There was, of course, no disguising of the fact that the Church of England denied the Papal claims. But given that denial, the 'golden mediocrity' commended by Archbishop Parker, the first Elizabethan bishop, was supposed to be inclusive of conservatives in doctrine and polity as well as those who had learnt much from their years of exile in the Reformed lands of the continent. This inclusiveness is the basis of the attraction exercised by the idea of the *Via Media*. The Church of England was, in the most obvious sense, protestant; but the important sense in which it was not merely protestant was contained in its hospitality to conservatism in doctrine and polity, a conservatism the importance of which grew with the years.[5] It is not therefore surprising that the explicit articulation of what, after all, is a traditional enough self-designation is peculiarly the work of Newman and the Tractarians. For Newman himself, the *Via Media* was not supposed to be an apologetic device for contemporary Anglicanism. It was rather an ideal for the Church of England, and to achieve it would mean some strenuous reformatory activities. In his most explicit Anglican writing on the topic, he admits that the *Via Media* has yet to be tried and is, hitherto, a matter of words on paper.

Hence there is a peculiar poignancy in his later account of the destruction of this ideal in his mind. The reasons he gives are largely the result of his reading of church history. Could the church really exist as a social institution in time and not change? Historical conditions impose on the church, as Newman saw it, the sheer necessity of developing; and the needs of the proclamation of the Gospel in such circumstances provide one with a prior expectation that the original revelation will be accompanied by the divine gift of an infallible developing authority. The *Via Media* is an impossibility. In due course men will be forced to choose between Catholicism or some sort of humanism.

. Although Tractarians continued to defend their understanding of the *Via Media* against Newman, his defection from the theory was a tremendous blow. Those who subsequently use the term do so, for the most part, merely as a way of speaking of Anglicanism's alleged moderation in a variety of respects. The term has no precise signification. This brief reference to the *Via Media* has two main points to it, therefore. In the first place it is a way of referring to the unique outcome of the Anglican reformation and its distinctive, but not unambiguous relationship to Roman Catholicism on the one hand and Protestantism on the other. Secondly, the circumstances in which the term became popular clearly suggest that the theory of the *Via Media*, if it is to be of any use whatsoever, is in need of very careful formulation. Indeed, the reformulation of the theory by F. D. Maurice is probably the principal way in which it is current today.

3. Thus the third of the four historical comments I propose to make on the background to the 1968 Lambeth statement on comphrehensiveness concerns the development, powerfully stimulated by the work of F. D. Maurice, of the idea of elements held in tension with each other. Maurice explicitly denied that the English church stood on 'an invisible equatorial line between Romanism and Protestantism'.[6] Instead of this he offers the view that the English church is a union of opposites, both of which are required for the completeness of truth, and for the practical tasks laid upon it. There are two features of Maurice's view of the matter which it is essential to bear in mind. The first was his whole-hearted commitment to the theory of national character and destiny which became popular in the early nineteenth century and had a substantial impact upon both German and English theology. This theory was part of the romantic idealist reaction against what was scorned as the facile internationalism of the Enlightenment. According to it, God is said to choose and to guide each nation, as he chose and guided the Jewish nation. Thirty years after Schleiermacher had himself condemned Anglomania among his compatriots we find Maurice thoroughly satisfied with the view that all true Germans *ought* to hate and denounce all German Anglomaniacs.[7] Every nation should seek to discover God's will and purpose for it, and to this task the national church of each nation should devote itself. The vision which he evidently cherished for the whole Church of Christ on earth was that of a united universal church, subdivided into national churches each reflecting in subordinate

particulars the individual characteristics of the different nations. Every such church would be at once 'catholic', in the sense of universal, and 'protestant', in the sense of acknowledging the sole Lordship of God.

On this feature of Maurice's theology Dr. Vidler comments with as much prescriptive as descriptive force, as follows:

> 'No one will be able to understand Maurice nor, what is more important, the English Church and the Anglican Communion, who supposes that the Catholic Church and National Churches are incompatible, or that as a Church becomes more Catholic it becomes less national, or who doubts that the Kingdom of Christ consecrates the life of nations . . .
>
> [The existence of the Anglican Communion] is a living protest on behalf of the principle of nationality and of the direct responsibility of bishops and rulers to Christ, and against the notion of a visible head of the Church and a centralised government.'[8]

This extraordinary annexation of the romantic nationalism of Maurice's theology to the very *raison d'etre* of Anglicanism destroys, of course, any right to claim that such Anglicanism preserves the essential principles of Catholicism in any sense which a Roman Catholic could possibly acknowledge. 'Catholicity' has been wholly redefined to fit a new, Anglican, theory of the church.

The second element of Maurice's theory that the Church of England has achieved not a middle course of compromise, but a union of opposites, is his well-known dislike for ecclesiastical parties. Indeed it amounts to an axiom of his thought, that if parties stand opposed to each other, then the truth of the matter lies with a hitherto unachieved reconciliation of all; he even applied this excessively synthetic theory to the Tory, Whig and Radical political schools of his day. The use of this axiom with reference to the ecclesiastical situation of his day involved two arguments; one, the denigration of the idea of a theological system and the claim that Anglicanism stood for no system, and, two, the assessment and criticism of each of the liberal, evangelical and catholic 'parties' in the Church of England. Maurice perceived, as is well known, that the logic of his position required that he also attack the idea that he was proposing a new, fourth, 'no party' party to oppose the other three.

What, then, according to Maurice, does Anglicanism stand for, if it stands for no system? Maurice's answer seems to have two sides to it. The first is that in Anglicanism there is an emphasis on what is practically effective, as distinct from what is said to be theoretically true; and secondly, consistent with the first, Anglicanism lays a stress on the ordinances of religion. In the *Kingdom of Christ* he wrote of the English reformation:

> 'Here the idea of the Church as a Spiritual Polity ruled over by Christ, and consisting of all baptized persons, did, owing to various providential circumstance, supersede the notion of a Church, as a sect, maintaining certain options; or to speak more correctly, the dogmatical side of Christianity was here felt to be its accessory and subordinate side, and the ordinances, which were the manifestation of it as the law of our social and practical life, were considered its principal side.'[9]

There is, in other words, an Anglican practice, but no specifically Anglican theory.

This influential interpretation of Maurice's view of Anglicanism has had a profound effect upon its official self-portraiture. The 1968 Lambeth Statement's denial that comprehensiveness is not compromise or syncretism has this stamp, as has the statement that the apprehension of truth is a 'growing thing'. In the 1948 Lambeth Conference, the Committee reporting on the Unity of the Church spoke in Mauricean tones of the tensions set up by different views of episcopacy.

> 'We recognise the inconveniences caused by these tensions, but we acknowledge them to be part of the will of God for us, since we believe it is only through a comprehensiveness which makes it possible to hold together in the Anglican Communion understandings of truth which are held in separation in other Churches, that the Anglican Communion is able to reach out in different directions and so to fulfil its special vocation as one of God's instruments for the restoration of the visible unit of His whole Church. If at the present time one view were to prevail to the exclusion of all others, we should be delivered from our tensions, but only at the price of missing our opportunity and our vocation.'[10]

With this we may compare words from an essay published by Vidler in the same year (1948), the year which also saw the publication of his book on Maurice.

> 'Anglican theology is true to its genius when it is seeking to reconcile opposed systems, rejecting them as exclusive systems, but showing that the principle for which each stands has its place within the total orbit of Christian truth, and in the long run is secure only within that orbit or (in the idiom of today)

when it is held in tension with other apparently opposed, but
really complementary, principles.'[11]

Historically speaking the appeal of Maurice's proposal is
obvious. Coined at a time when internal party strife was at its
most acute, it apparently offered a non-partisan refuge for that
large body of central Anglicans who properly speaking belonged
to no party, neither evangelical, nor high church, nor yet in any
committed sense to the more radical of the liberals. Theologically
speaking, however, the effect of the proposal has been disastrous.
It must be said bluntly that it has served as an open invitation
to intellectual laziness and self-deception. Maurice's opposition
to system-building has proved a marvellous excuse to those who
believe they can afford to be condescending about the outstanding theological contribution of theologians from other
communions and smugly tolerant of second-rate theological
competence in our own; and the failure to be frank about
the issues between the parties in the Church of England has led
to an ultimately illusory self-projection as a Church without any
specific doctrinal or confessional position.

But it is specifically with respect to the principle of the
complementarity of apparently opposed truths that Maurice's
position is most questionable. Lots of contradictory things may
be said to be complementary by those with a vested interest in
refusing to think straight. What complementarity requires, if it
it so to be used in a *rational* manner, is the demonstration that
both of the alleged truths are true and necessary to the proper
depiction of the reality being studied. And there is a great dif-
ference between saying that a body like a church has found it
practically possible to contain people who hold opposed and
contradictory views, and saying that that church believes that
all of the contradictory views are true and in some hitherto un-
discovered way reconcilable. Those who, for whatever reason,
have decided that the latter view is a more respectable version
of the comprehensiveness of the Church of England, have
regrettably followed Maurice in covert redefinition of the terms
such as 'catholic' and 'protestant'. It is, of course, the easiest
thing in the world to 'hold together' views labelled respectively
'catholic', 'protestant' (and even 'liberal') by a suitable process
of emasculation of controversial content. And it is greatly to be
feared that generations of Anglicans, learning their theories
from Maurice and his disciples, have substituted for the form of

catholicism or protestantism which any convinced believer of these respective forms of Christian discipleship would recognise a tame and Anglicanised *tertium quid*.

4. The final historical observation concerns one extremely important episode in the modern history of Anglicanism, namely the transition from tractarianism to liberal catholicism in the nineteenth century. One of the major features of the contemporary Church of England is the evident decay of anglo-catholicism, bewildered alike by the changes in the Roman church and the extreme theological radicalism of some whose style and sympathies are evidently more catholic than evangelical. The historical progression from a frankly reactionary tractarianism to a measure of accommodation with liberal theological scholarship is thus an important element in the analysis of the contemporary Anglican church, and it is of great importance to the articulation of a theory of comprehensiveness.

The obvious figure to consider as representative of the liberal catholic standpoint is Charles Gore (1853-1932), though, as we shall see, the position he adopted and the method he used were quite quickly discarded by those who followed in his steps. The question what form of accommodation he could achieve with contemporary liberalism is most frequently answered by reference to his contributions to *Lux Mundi* (1889, and the Preface to the tenth edition of 1890). Here, and in his subsequent publications on christology, Gore showed that he was quite willing to bring forward theories unknown or contradictory to those of the Fathers, provided that none of the early councils had made any definitive pronouncements on the issues involved. However, when faced with a noxious example of radical theological liberalism, the so-called 'New Theology' of R. J. Campbell, which cast doubt on the articles of the creed, Gore's reaction was intransigent; and it is this response which is of most interest in assessing the limits of his preparedness to allow theological liberalism in the Church of England.

In an age of change, criticism and new knowledge Gore was acutely concerned to defend the view that 'permanent Christianity' meant the faith summarised and expressed in the catholic creeds. No-one who did not *ex animo* believe these creeds ought to be allowed to minister to a Church of England congregation. Belief in the central creeds of Christendom, general acceptance of and willingness to use the formularies and services of the Church of England, and a promise to teach out of the Scriptures are the three bases for doctrinal unity and the source of the church's comprehensiveness, its capacity to embrace different schools of thought.[12] At the same time Gore expressed himself fully satisfied that biblical criticism left unaffected any of the articles of the creed. The faith of the creeds, he believed, was, in fact, supported by free inquiry into historical facts, and he explained the negative results of certain critics as arising from their non-historical presuppositions, such as disbelief in the possibility of miracles.

Gore allows that the Christian theist might himself well be said to approach the evidence for biblical miracles with presuppositions. But this, he considered, was both proper and inevitable. What his position amounted to was this: Only that man could minister in the Church of England who was persuaded that the evidence against any article of the creed was not strong enough to dissuade him from believing it, as one who approached the matter with a theistic frame of reference. Gore did not defend the infallibility of scripture; what he did defend was the absolute authority of the Apostles' and Nicene creeds for the ministry of the Church of England. To the laity he was prepared to give a measure of latitude, but none to the clergy. Integrity demanded that if they felt obliged, on historical or other grounds, to doubt the credal miracles they must resign their orders. At the time, however, there were many prominent clergy in the Church of England who disagreed, both with Gore's general view of Anglican discipline and also with his historical views on the results of biblical scholarship. There were also those who were prepared to say, as did Hensley Henson, that they believed the words of the creed *ex animo*, meaning by that that they believed what they took to be its essential meaning.[13] That is to say, they claimed for themselves liberty of interpretation about the 'essential point' made by any credal proposition. With reference to the virgin birth or the resurrection this might very well be something other than the factual or physical miracle, clearly believed in by the compilers of the creeds or some of the authors of the New Testament documents.

Gore, however, described his own position as that of liberal Catholicism, and meant by it in fact nothing more nor less than Anglicanism itself.[14] Moreover, modern Anglicans are to be found who regard Gore's liberality of outlook as the hallmark of historic Anglicanism, the application in the circumstances of the late nineteenth- and early twentieth centuries of the identical theological method of the 'classic' Anglicanism of the seventeenth century.[15] But how 'liberal' was Gore? Bishop Michael Ramsey rightly asked the question in his influential interpretation of Anglican thought, *From Gore to Temple*: 'If criticism is allowed to modify thus far the presentation of the faith, what if criticism questions the substance of the faith as the creeds affirm it?'[16]

Gore's viewpoint on this issue was that criticism would not question the credal substance of the faith, and that the Church of England was secure in maintaining that it did not. On both counts he was wrong; on what grounds, therefore, is his 'liberality' held up as a model of the Anglican method of theology in operation? Vidler, Ramsey and McAdoo all readily admit that, temperamentally speaking, Gore was not a liberal-minded individual and that there was a streak of fanaticism in his character. But this does not help us in the assessment of his theological method, in particular of the position he accorded to the creeds in an area of critical biblical study. The fact is that, far from adopting a uniquely Anglican stance, Gore was defending a position which a German Lutheran pastor, Melchior Goetze, had adopted over a hundred years earlier in a controversy with Lessing. He was trying to use historical argument to support a position which had never been adopted for historical reasons, and in doing so he was necessarily making it vulnerable. As Lessing observed against Goetze, the orthodox faith on matters such as the virgin birth or the resurrection was not proclaimed as a result of exhaustive historical inquiry into the evidence, and to defend it by historical argument is to admit that objections based on historical reasoning provide sufficient ground for doubt. The importance of this view lies in its implication for the church's understanding of dogma. Once it is admitted that historical evidence is relevant to dogma, then the question is naturally what right a church has to prescribe the results of historical inquiry. Gore's position was exactly that of Goetze, namely that historical argument has to be used to defend dogma, and that historical inquiry when carried out does support the church's dogmatic faith.

Nonetheless, Gore's position could be described as liberal in two senses. He was prepared, against the older tractarian principle, to allow that new knowledge might lead to 'great changes in the outlying departments of theology', by which some of the views of the fathers might have been corrected.[17] Liddon correctly perceived that abandonment of belief in the infallibility of Scripture, and Gore's proposal about Jesus' limitations in knowledge, were theological novelties contrary to the older tractarian belief, and, more importantly, innovatory in method. Secondly, Gore was liberal to the extent that he placed so much stress on the conclusions of historical scholarship. True he insisted that biblical study raised acutely the the question of the historian's attitude to the miraculous, and that decisions taken on this issue affected the theologian's whole understanding of the nature of history and of God's dealings with mankind. But in principle the biblical documents were not immune from historical probing; Gore's argument was that they had been probed, and found to be generally trustworthy.

But the question he did not tackle satisfactorily was whether a Church could demand that all its clergy adopt the same conclusions on historical matters. In view of the very large quantity and weight of dissentient voices in Gore's own day and since, it would be a little absurd to claim that Gore's position on this matter was in any sense characteristically Anglican. Indeed it was at once dropped by the next generation of Anglicans in Gore's tradition, men like Rawlinson, Knox, Figgis and Selwyn.[18]

Rawlinson especially made it clear that he believed there were no good grounds for distinguishing between clergy and laity in the public profession of the creed of the church.[19] Two quotations from a sermon he preached in 1925 indicate a quite different response to the whole matter of the liberal challenge.

'Belief in the principle of liberty does not mean simply belief in the liberty of those with whom one happens to be in personal agreement. It means the refusal to have the church turned into a sect, or administered by methods of discipline analogous to those which obtain in the Church of Rome.

Any and every particular manifestation or expression of the Church ... —for example, the Church of England — ought ... to aim at being Catholic, in the sense of being comprehensive of all that is Christian. It ought to aim at excluding none whom our Lord Jesus Christ would not exclude. It ought to rule out in principle no type of thought

> or of temperament, and no forms of devotion, which are in any sense genuinely and defensibly Christian.'[20]

It is this response, rather than Gore's, which bears the stamp of an appropriate response to the phenomena of biblical criticism and historical study. But the obvious question it raises is how *anything* in the extremely wide range of post-enlightenment liberal Christian theology could be excluded. How could one show that some of the more novel suggestions in radical theological thought were in no sense 'genuinely and defensibly Christian'? There are, moreover, ecclesiastical questions to be asked. On what grounds could one exclude practising non-conformists from eucharistic fellowship of such a truly comprehensive and catholic church? These are the questions which must be faced if Rawlinson's more liberal position is adopted. But the very liberality of the proposal involves complexities which the mere notion of comprehensiveness is powerless to resolve.

FOOTNOTES

1. On recent discussion with Orthodox churchmen, see the account by Metropolitan Methodios of Aksum in *Ekklesiastikos Pharos*, Vol. LV, 1 (1973), pp. 5-38
2. The Lambeth Conference 1968 (London, 1968), p. 140
3. From his *The Religion of Protestants* (1637), cited in P. E. More and F. L. Cross, Anglicanism (London, 1935) p. 113. See the essay by More in the same volume on 'The Spirit of Anglicanism', pp. xxivff, , and H. R. McAdoo, *The Spirit of Anglicanism*, (London, 1965) pp. 375ff.
4. For example in A. T. P. Williams, *The Anglican Tradition in the Life of England* (London, 1947) p. 20
5. O. Chadwick, *The Mind of the Oxford Movement* (London, 1960), p.16
6. *The Kingdom of Christ* (Everyman Edition) II, p. 311, cited by A. R. Vidler, *The Theology of F. D. Maurice* (London, 1945). Chapter 8 of this book, entitled 'A United Confession of the Name', is the source for much of what follows.
7. *The Kingdom of Christ* (1838), III, p. 377, cited in Vidler, *The Theology of F. D. Maurice*, p. 190
8. *The Theology of F. D. Maurice*, p. 215
9. II, p. 338, cited in Vidler, *The Theology of F. D. Maurice*, p. 214
10. *The Lambeth Conference 1948* (London, 1948), Part II, pp. 50f
11. *Essays in Liberality* (London, 1957) pp. 166f
12. *The New Theology and the Old Religion* (London, 1908) pp. 162-167 and p. 228
13. See A. M. Ramsey, *From Gore to Temple* (London, 1960), pp. 88ff, and J. C. Livingston, *The Ethics of Belief*. An Essay on the Victorian Religious Conscience (Tallahassee, Florida, 1974), pp. 47ff
14. Cf. James Carpenter, *Gore*, A Study in Liberal Catholic Thought (London 1960), ch. 2
15. Thus More, in More and Cross, *op. cit*, and especially Bishop H. R. McAdoo in *The Spirit of Anglicanism*, p.v. and pp. 152-155

16. *From Gore to Temple,* p. 14; see also Alec Vidler's essay, 'Bishop Gore and Liberal Catholicism', in *Essays in Liberality* (London, 1957), p. 126

17. Preface to *Lux Mundi* (1889)

18. See the essays on 'Authority' by A. E. Rawlinson and W. L. Knox in *Essays Catholic and Critical* (London, 1926). Also the comments of Bishop Ramsey, *From Gore to Temple,* pp. 101-106, and A. R. Vidler, *20th Century Defenders of the Faith* (London, 1965) ch. 3

19. A. E. J. Rawlinson, *Dogma, Fact and Experience* (London, 1915) pp. 196ff

20. A. E. J. Rawlinson, *Freedom within the Church* (Cambridge, 1928) pp. 6 and 10, cited from Vidler, *Essays in Liberality,* pp. 147f. Rawlinson's reference to the exclusion of no type of temperament is reminiscent of J. N. Figgis who had traced the party divisions of the Church of England to differences of temperament, in a sermon on 'Anglican Comprehensiveness' in *Hopes for English Religion* (London, 1919) p.88

Chapter 2

THE SIGNIFICANCE OF LIBERALISM

SO far I have almost self-consciously averted my gaze from the modernists in the Church of England. I have done this deliberately, because, so far as I know, no-one has ever suggested that the modernist movement is really the core of the Church of England, in the way in which a generation of scholars have set out to canonise the liberal catholics. Modernists, indeed, have suffered from a rather absurdly bad press. Michael Ramsey sets out to show that the theological views of modernists like Rashdall and Bethune-Baker proved to be but a temporary phenomenon linked as it was to a heterodox doctrine of the relation of God and man. Roger Lloyd asserted that the biblical work of Sir Edwyn Hoskyns achieved the 'eclipse of Liberalism', and exploded 'the Liberal Protestant fallacy'. [1] The time has come to consider the impact which the modernists had on the Church of England, especially in relation to the question of the breadth of theological view permissible in its teachers.

It is perfectly reasonable to regard the English modernists in the first instance as constituting the Anglican wing of the European movement of liberal protestantism, which was of such power and importance at the turn of the century. [2] The Modern Churchmen's Union, known until 1928 as the Churchmen's Union, was specifically formed to provide a platform for liberal religious opinion in the Church of England, and the rather heterogeneous collections of leaders in that body were to a considerable degree united in their opposition to, and dislike of, the specific doctrines and practices of high churchmen. It was to be expected that many of those who claimed the right to reinterpret aspects of traditional Christian doctrine in the light of biblical research or of modern philosophy or science found refuge in this cave of Adullam. Many of its members were far from radical, however. William Sanday (1843-1920) is an interesting example of a very moderate English liberal protestant in the Anglican church. Sanday was a scholar who set himself the task of acquiring the necessary critical skills for writing a life of Christ, including a thorough immersion in the substantial German literature on the subject. Sanday had the reputation in

England of being a liberal theologian, partly because of his hesitations about the virgin birth. But unlike many of the German scholars of moderate liberal protestant persuasion, the so-called right-wing Ritschlians, he wanted to defend the creeds, the doctrine of the incarnation and the idea of doctrinal continuity — all highly Anglican doctrinal traits. Aware that he himself would be regarded as a typical *Vermittelungstheologe* (a theologian mediating between confessionalism and liberalism) he nevertheless sought strenuously to depict his own position as in some sense uniquely Anglican, deploying arguments of a rather rhetorical and impressionistic kind to support his obviously Anglican confessional preferences. A number of letters exist between him and German liberal protestants where these different emphases are noted. When one considers how heated was the discussion, in Sanday's day, of the Anglican problem of clerical assent to the articles of the creed, one can well appreciate how strongly he felt compelled as someone regarded as an authority on the dangerous tradition of German biblical scholarship, to differentiate his position from theirs. Sanday does defend an Anglican type of position, but his general theological stance is intelligible only as a minor regional variant of that of many German liberal protestants, and in what follows that is how the Anglican modernists are regarded.[3]

What emerges from a study of the liberal protestants with whom Sanday was connected is that many of them consider themselves to be mediators between hard line orthodoxy and wild radicalism. They did not regard themselves in the first instance as theological innovators. This is true of a liberal protestant like Harnack, who knew himself to be outflanked theologically by men who portrayed Jesus as an eschatological prophet finally disappointed of his hope. It is true also of those modern churchmen who set themselves the task of reinterpreting christology at the notorious Modern Churchmen's Union Conference at Girton College, Cambridge in 1921. Far from hoping or intending to shock the orthodox in the wearisome manner of a group of middle-aged radicals, the modern churchmen had it in mind to provide an alternative to the rather bleak implications for christology of some recent biblical study by some fellow modernists, F. J. Foakes Jackson and K. Lake.[4] Because the methods exemplified at the conference by some of the modernist speakers tended to differ from those who accepted Chalcedonian orthodoxy as a datum for christological thought, and also because some of their conclusions were either novel or ambiguous, orthodox incarnationalists descended on them in fury.

The importance of the events to which this conference gave rise is universally admitted. Gore's reaction to it is most instructive. He believed, and had believed for some time, that the modernists were intent on undermining the authority of the creeds (which was, in his view, the same thing as undermining the basis of the Church of England), and he demanded that this latest exhibition of the drift towards Unitarianism be subject to ecclesiastical discipline. Otherwise, he thought, it would be said that the teaching of the modernists had achieved the status of a school of thought within the Church of England.[5] Gore was in fact outmanoeuvred on this issue by the extremely experienced Archbishop of Canterbury, Randall Davidson; and the steps taken to quieten the whole furore included the setting up of a Commission on Christian doctrine with the following terms of reference:

> 'To consider the nature and grounds of Christian doctrine with a view to demonstrating the extent of existing agreement within the Church of England and with a view to investigating how far it is possible to remove or diminish existing differences.'[6]

In October of 1925 the Commission, headed after the death of Bishop Burge by Bishop William Temple, reported on the emergence of a greater degree of unanimity than might have been anticipated and on the success of the group in showing the complementarity of views often regarded as divergent.[7] But the nearest the commission comes to a direct reply to Gore's protest that modernism should be excluded as a 'school of thought' occurs in Temple's introduction to the report, where he wrote:

> 'The Anglican Churches have received and hold the faith of Catholic Christendom, but they have exhibited a rich variety in methods both of approach and of interpretation. They are the heirs of the Reformation as well as of Catholic tradition; and they hold together in a single fellowship of worship and witness those whose chief attachment is to each of these, and also those whose attitude to the distinctively Christian tradition of a free and liberal culture which is historically the bequest of the Greek spirit and was recovered for Western Europe at the Renaissance.'

The wording of this statement demands careful consideration. The addition of 'the tradition of a free and liberal culture' to the customary duality of catholic and protestant elements within the Anglican church does, of course, no less than justice to the very longstanding and once powerful tradition of latitudinarian or broad churchmanship.[8] It is to them that Anglicans chiefly owe their early deliverance from the sterility and bitterness of much post-reformation theological debate. But Temple does not distinguish within this tradition of liberalism between the earlier and the later phase. For when biblical criticism took hold of theological education by the middle of the nineteenth century an emphatic change overtook the character of Anglican liberalism. Whereas in the earlier period a latitudinarian divine might very well appeal to the simplicity and diversity of scripture against the complexity and uniform rigour of subsequent dogmatic orthodoxy, the biblical critic subjected the Bible itself to liberal interpretation. It can hardly be the case that Temple was unaware of the importance of this critical advance. He certainly must have known, since it had been repeatedly discussed, that if certain clear affirmations of both bible and creed were subjected to criticism and became matters of dubiety (such as the virgin birth) it became difficult to see where the process would stop. The advantage of believing in the existence of fundamentals and non-fundamentals (as did the latitudinarians), was that you could say precisely that criticism or doubt stopped at the fundamentals.

The modernists are in a very different position. When one of the most weighty of them, Hastings Rashdall, faced the question, what are the essential and what the inessential doctrines, he was forced to admit that he regarded the matter as insoluble in the terms in which it was posed. Though he could think of many opinions which it would be undesirable for a man to hold as a clergyman of the Church of England, each man, he believed, had to face the question for himself (in consultation, if need be, with his bishop). The resolution of the issue could not be predetermined; it was a matter of spiritual expediency in the light of the climate of opinion of his day. Rashdall thought that he himself would draw the line at doubt of theism and human immortality, and at any unwillingness to recognise the uniqueness of the Christian revelation such that the ordinary language of the church about the divinity of Christ could only be used with a feeling of unreality.[9] One need hardly say that this kind of degree of liberalism was totally unacceptable to Gore. But was Temple's smooth and ambiguous phrase about 'the tradition of a free and liberal culture' meant to exclude or include it?

One thing that must be said is that the liberalism of the doctrine report itself is disciplined and moderate. On the precise question of christology which had been raised by the Girton conference, the report is most circumspect. There have always been, it says, two main tendencies in christology; one which seeks to 'do justice to' (a phrase of truly formidable ambiguity) the true humanity, another to the true divinity of Jesus Christ. If developed in a one-sided way, each of these 'is destructive of the full truth of the Incarnation ' (p.75). The Incarnation is, indeed, the presuppostion of the whole section, and the writers believe themselves to be simply reformulating that truth which has been revealed and remains unchanged. On the vexed question of clerical assent to the creeds the greatest difficulty had obviously been experienced by the commission, and a most carefully phrased seven point resolution defining the acceptable limits of dissent was drawn up (see Appendix). A note indicated that some members considered that too wide a latitude had been given to those who did not teach or believe the doctrine traditional in the church.

Despite the evident ambiguity (or even because of it), the outcome of the report must be said to be an unambiguous victory for the liberals. The unappetising prospect of widespread use of the church's cumbersome and objectionable disciplinary machinery against respected figures of the academic and clerical establishment doubtless encouraged the members of the commission to find some way of accommodating the newer form of liberalism within the Anglican communion. But the position which they adopted was characterised by an ultimately unhelpful lack of clarity about the nature of liberalism itself, ostensibly the very cause of the whole inquiry. For the liberalism which the report did nothing to set aside, even if it included it within the scope of Anglican comprehensiveness in a suitably muted and ambiguous form, cannot be merely *added* to the ingredients of Anglicanism. The temptation to do this is all but irresistible. After all liberalism is an -ism like evangelical-ism or anglo-catholic-ism; and there is a long tradition of speaking of three

parties in the Church of England, one of whom is the broad
church or liberal party. Moreover the modernists did, in the end,
form themselves into a group, held conferences and published
a journal, all traditional party activities.

But it is a mistake to leap to conclusions in this matter. It
is admitted by all that the modernists of the 1920s were never
more than a coalition, held together by the need to stand
against some very powerful forces which would have hunted
them out of the Church of England given half a chance. And it
is evident, now, that with the threat removed, the so-called
movement or party lacks any clear direction. It is a very obvious
fact that modern radicals in the Church of England neither form
a cohesive group nor identify themselves with the earlier
modernist movement.

What then of the earlier broad churchman, the so-called
latitudinarians? Here the answer must be that, while it makes
sense to speak of this group as a party in the seventeenth and
early eighteenth century and while their influence is felt in the
nineteenth, the breadth of theological investigation introduced
by the biblical critics utterly changes the picture. Nineteenth-
century liberalism differs fundamentally from seventeenth-
century latitudinarianism in respect of its attitude to the Bible.
Liberalism in the later sense simply meant giving up the long-
treasured doctrine of the inerrancy of the Bible, and submitting
the scriptures to literary and historical criticism. In this sense,
of course, one could only be either a liberal or an obscurantist,
and it must not be forgotten that there were very many of the
latter in the nineteenth-century Church of England. But did
liberalism by itself imply the adoption of any particular theological party stance? Maurice believed so, and attributed to the
liberals a variety of opinions with which he himself disagreed,
such as a desire to abandon the Prayer Book and the Articles, to
create a synthesis with nineteenth-century 'superstitions', to be
opposed to all forms of theology and to be tolerant of all theological opinions.[10] It would not be wholly fair to dismiss this
as a piece of typical Mauricean eccentricity. There were
individual theologians who held one or other of these views and
whom it would be right to speak of as liberal. But to attribute
them *en masse* to a 'party' is to mythologise on the grand
scale; and the reason for such cavalier inventiveness is that
Maurice's theory required that there should be a liberal party

which had grasped a facet of the truth but which erred grievously as a system. Sadly it is the case that whole flocks of writers on 'liberalism' in the Church of England have followed Maurice's example of constructing a single figure of straw out of the very great diversity of liberal opinion.

What then is 'liberalism' or the 'liberal viewpoint'? Perhaps the sharpest way of answering this question is simply to deny that liberals have a viewpoint on doctrinal matters in the sense in which evangelicals or anglo-catholics do. To this extent at least T. S. Eliot was correct; liberalism is a negative phenomenon, a finding of the courage and the grounds *not* to hold views frequently held in the past and invested, it may be, with the venerable authority of tradition. The point is well made by Eliot that neither liberalism nor conservatism are philosophies, *per se*, that both may be habits of mind, and that both may lead to disaster when mistaken for something positive.[11] Liberalism in Christian theology can only operate by challenging the familiar authorities, whatever they may happen to be. But it does not itself stand for or profess any one philosophy or set of doctrines, other than the doctrine that theological proposals are not true because they are traditional. The attempt to ascribe to liberalism some principle of the self-sufficiency of reason is monstrously unfair, as is the accusation that liberal theologies are necessarily anthropocentric.

If defined in such a broad way there are two main consequences. The first is that a 'liberal' theological proposal is always in the form of a challenge to an established authority, and thus necessarily implies a dispute about the appropriate norms or criteria for any theology whatsoever. And the second consequence is that it is impossible merely to be a 'liberal' in theology. If one's theology has any distinguishing character at all, it will be liberal in as much as it is a modification of an already existing type. It will, in other words, be liberal catholic, or liberal evangelical, or (and this I believe to be an appropriate designation for a discernible type of theology) liberal latitudinarian.

What, however, seems not to have been recognised by Temple, nor is it recognised by a host of other writers subsequently, is that liberalism is a cuckoo in the Anglican nest, and that the all-too facile inclusion of it under the guise of a 'party' with a long and honoured history in Anglicanism was bound to be no more than a temporary measure. If liberalism always has the instinct to challenge established authorities, no church which has once admitted that authorities can and should be interrogated will be able to devise an unchallengeable basis for itself. It will never be immune from internal debate and from the clash of opposed opinion. And this opinion may be *really opposed,* without any guarantee that all the expressed opinions are in some ineffable sense necessary to a higher truth. Persons, in such a case, will hold views which are contradictory of, not complementary to, those of other persons in the same church. Maurice's notion of comprehensiveness is utterly inadequate to account for this situation, and to persist in using it is a dangerous form of ecclesiastical self-deception. Some other account of a church which permits its members to be liberal (in this sense) must be given, and it is to this task that I believe Anglicans must bend their energies without delay if they hope that the actual situation in their communion be taken seriously by the world-wide Church.

The negative impact of liberalism in theology is nowhere more sharply evident than in the recent report of the Doctrine Commission of the Church of England on *Christian Believing.* From the standpoint of this book what is most interesting is that the principle of complementarity comes directly under attack. Christians, the report recognises, do not agree about the meaning or the truth of the propositions of the creeds. It lists four main, and divergent, attitudes towards the problem of the use of creeds in the contemporary church and analyses the basic differences. It comments:

> 'The issues here — on the one hand loyalty to the formulas of the church and obedience to received truth, on the other adventurous exploration and the Church's engagement with the contemporary world — appear to point in very different directions and to reflect different conceptions of the nature of religious truth. It is, to say the least, very difficult to explain divergences of this fundamental kind merely as complementary aspects of the many-sided wisdom of God.'[12]

This confrontation of mutually exclusive views the report proposes has to be handled in a new manner. Weariness or distress may suggest that one or other attitude ought to be ruled out as inconsistent with Christian discipleship. But, the report continues,

> 'we are convinced that any such decision would be disastrous

> to the health of the Church. The tension must be endured.
> What is important is that everything should be done (and
> suffered) to make it a creative tension — that is, not a state of
> non-communication between mutually embattled groups but
> one of constant dialogue with consequent cross-fertilization of
> ideas and insight (p. 38).'

Furthermore, the report believes that this dialogue is qualitatively
conditioned by its taking place in the total context of 'the community of faith', by an ever-renewed engagement with the 'classical tradition' of Christian faith including scriptures and creeds,
and by an openness to truth from whatever quarter it may
come.

Whatever the weaknesses of this crucial section of the
report, and they are considerable as I hope to show, in one very
important respect it is a substantial clarification of the real
situation in the contemporary Church of England; indeed, the
situation as it has been for a very considerable time. If my
argument is correct what it signals is the end of a bogus theory
of comprehensiveness, which for far too long has lain like a fog
over the Anglican mind. Of course, it is quite understandable
how the notion of comprehensiveness developed out of the
Elizabethan settlement, at a time when the *limits* of such
comprehensiveness could be set by agreement on the articles of
the creed. The exacerbation of the conflict between evangelical
and anglo-catholic in the nineteenth century gave rise, again
understandably, to the theory of the complementarity of both
viewpoints to a greater truth. It was a theory with an irresistible
attraction for bishops endeavouring to achieve a *modus vivendi*
between warring groups in their dioceses. And if, by sleight of
hand, the new liberalism of theological education could be
transformed into another party, and assimilated to a relatively
innocuous party out of the Anglican past, then it would seem
that there had only been a slight modification of the party
situation in Anglicanism. But this was never the truth, and it
seems that a major portion of the blame must rest upon Maurice
and his confused and misleading account of the party situation
in the nineteenth-century Church of England. It must be said
bluntly that the militant tractarian and the militant protestant
saw the matter more accurately. The painful series of law suits
in which they engaged was the real battlefield where the future
of the Church of England was decided; and if in the end they
learnt to co-exist, it was principally because, as many power-

groups have discovered before and since, the adverse practical results of judicial conflict were ultimately more detrimental to their respective causes among the uncommitted. The offensiveness of Maurice's theory was that it depicted party men as somehow disloyal to the church by reason of their one-sidedness. But 'the church' of Maurice was a paper church, a figment of his imagination and not the Church of England, where men had the right to call contradiction by its proper name.

In conclusion, the significance of liberalism can be briefly portrayed. It means quite simply that there will always be those who will claim the right to challenge what may have become the received view in the Anglican church. It means, in fact, that there will always be doctrinal conflict. But because liberal theologians do not constitute a party, there should never be any attempt either to assimilate or to reject them *en masse*. To accept the inevitability of some liberals, does not necessitate the toleration of all. Views are neither right nor wrong by being liberal in character. Only a church which had despaired of the possibility of rational argument about theology altogether could adopt such a stance. And it is my conviction that, tolerant though the Anglican communion has become, it has a standpoint on matters of doctrine which is firmer than seems to be the case at first sight, even if it stands in need of articulation and development.

FOOTNOTES

1. *The Church of England, 1900-1965* (London, 1966), pp. 271ff.
2. As does O. C. Quick in his perceptive *Liberalism, Modernism and Tradition* (London, 1922), p. 5, and also Vidler in a note on the modern churchmen in *20th Century Defenders of the Faith* (London, 1965), pp. 123f.
3. See his *Life of Christ in Recent Research* (London, 1907), esp. p. 182
4. See *The Modern Churchman XI* (1921), pp. 201-348
5. See G. L. Prestige, *The Life of Charles Gore* (London, 1935), pp. 455ff and G.K.A. Bell, *Randall Davidson* (3rd ed. Oxford, 1952), p. 1141
6. *Doctrine in the Church of England,* The Report of the Commission on Christian Doctrine appointed by the Archbishops of Canterbury and York in 1922 (London, 1938), p. 19
7. *The Times,* Friday October 1925, cited in H. D. A. Major, *English Modernism* (Harvard, 1927), pp. 254ff
8. On the importance of Cambridge Platonists and the Latitudinarians, see G. R. Cragg, *From Puritanism to the Age of Reason* (Cambridge, 1966) chs. III and. IV
9. *Anglican Liberalism,* by twelve Churchmen (London, 1908), p. 106
10. See A. R. Vidler, *The Theology of F. D. Maurice,* p. 218
11. *The Idea of a Christian Society* (London, 1939) p. 17
12. *Christian Believing* (London, 1976), p. 38

Chapter 3

THE ANGLICAN STANDPOINT?

I PROPOSE in this section of the book to take up in a more systematic way the problem of the responsibility which the Anglican church has for making clear its doctrinal standpoint. The debate about a greater measure of freedom for clergy to interpret, or even to dissent from, the contents of the Book of Common Prayer, the Ordinal and the Thirty· Nine Articles passed through a number of stages. In 1975 a new form of assent was authorised, which replaced one drawn up in 1865, and which is now read in the Church of England by those being ordained or taking up church office, including some laymen. Since it bears so closely on Anglican self-understanding it is worth quoting in full. It consists of two parts, a preface read by the person requiring the declaration (usually the bishop) and the declaration itself:

> '*Preface*
> The Church of England is part of the One, Holy, Catholic and Apostolic Church worshipping the one true God, Father, Son and Holy Spirit. It professes the faith uniquely revealed in the Holy Scriptures and set forth in the catholic creeds, which faith the Church is called upon to proclaim afresh in each generation. Led by the Holy Spirit, it has borne witness to Christian truth in its historic formularies, the Thirty-nine Articles of Religion, the Book of Common Prayer and the Ordering of Bishops, Priests and Deacons. In the declaration you are about to make will you affirm your loyalty to this inheritance of faith as your inspiration and guidance under God in bringing the grace and truth of Christ to this generation and making Him known to those in your care.
> *Declaration of Assent*
> I, A.B., do so affirm and accordingly declare my belief in the faith which is revealed in the Holy Scriptures and set forth in the catholic creeds and to which the historic formularies of the Church of England bear witness; and in public prayer and administration of the sacraments, I will use only the forms of service which are authorised or allowed by Canon.'

One effect of this new declaration is to dispense the clergy of the Church of England from the need to examine themselves closely as regards their assent to the Thirty Nine Articles, a process which has caused many candidates for ordination, for many years, considerable difficulty. The reference to 'loyalty to this inheritance of faith as your inspiration and guidance under God' provides the one making the declaration of assent with considerable liberty of interpretation. Nonetheless, both in the preface and in the declaration itself belief is required and given to the faith 'uniquely revealed in the Holy Scriptures and set forth in the catholic creeds', and it was to the exploration of the nature of this faith and its expression in Holy Scripture and the creeds that the Doctrine Commission devoted itself in its Report of 1976.

It is frequently said of the reports of the Doctrine Commissions that they deal with *doctrine in*, not the *doctrine of*, the Church of England. This remark is true enough, and certainly minimises (as it intends to) the authority of such documents. It is also true, however, that if a report is commissioned and received, it has value as a statement of what opinion is at least found tolerable in the Church of England — that is, provided no steps are taken to suppress it. The 1976 Report is remarkable for one particular feature, namely that whereas a bare 42 pages contain the agreed statement (and of these a considerable number are devoted to descriptions of divergent views), 114 pages are devoted to signed appendices or individual essays. Despite the radicalism of at least some of the essays, one is clearly intended to believe that none of them fall outside the limits of the 'creative tension' (quoted above), which the main body of the Report espoused. The position at the end of the day is that if a young ordinand can identify himself with one or other of the views described or championed in such a work, it can hardly be said to him that his view is not consistent with the position of the Church of England. To this extent at least it can be said that these documents provide guidelines in interpreting the stance of the Church of England.

If we put together the 1975 Declaration of Assent and the 1976 Report on Christian Believing the position seems, then, to be somewhat as follows. The Church of England corporately professes the faith uniquely revealed in the Holy Scriptures and set forth in the catholic creeds, but will find no difficulty in ordaining or commissioning persons who have serious reservations about credal beliefs or who regard them as mistaken, provided they can take the declaration of assent.[1] But how could such persons affirm and declare their 'belief in the faith which is revealed in the Holy Scriptures and set forth in the catholic creeds'? The answer lies in a distinction between theology and faith. Belief is not said to be in the theological propositions of Holy Scripture or the theological propositions of the creeds, but in the faith 'revealed in' Holy Scripture and 'set forth in' the catholic creeds. Both Scripture and creeds may be said to be *vehicles* of the faith, a faith which, it may be thought, needs to be reformulated in the present. It seems that the precise wording of the Declaration of Assent, though it reads as a rather firm profession of faith, could not be said to exclude a very liberal interpretation. If that is so, then it is vital to add that the same is true of the church's *corporate* profession of faith. That too is capable of liberal interpretation; indeed by stating that the church is called on to procalim this faith 'afresh in each gener- ation' the preface to the declaration positively invites the construction that novelties are to be expected in such pro- clamation. 'Afresh' is, of course, ambiguous, and could as well mean 'the same thing, but time and time again' as it could mean 'with ever new insight and vocabulary'. This ambiguity is, as we have noted, not uncharacteristic of the response of the Church of England to the phenomenon of liberalism in theology.

Are there then no boundaries to the degree to which the Church of England is prepared to tolerate diversity of doctrinal conviction? Here the Report on Christian Believing claims to have offered a suggestion which certainly ought to be taken seriously. The members of the Commission have tried to show, they state,

> 'that underlying even very widely differing presentations of Christian faith there is in fact a common pattern or method of thinking, varying certainly in emphasis from one case to another but concerned in the last analysis with the same ingredients; and to suggest that the vital requirement for Christians today is not to force themselves to specifically agreed   conclusions but to operate within the pattern — that is, to use in whatever way or proportion integrity allows the resources which the Christian community makes available. (p.5)'

This statement needs to be taken seriously, but it scarcely deserves to be handled with undue reverence. What, it needs to be asked, is this pattern or method of thinking, and how does it arise from concern with 'the resources which the Christian community makes available'? There are several possibilities.

First, by the 'ingredients' which are the concern of Christian thinking it could be that the commission has in mind the data of the history of the Christian church in Scripture and tradition. But this will not do, since the interpretation of the data by a Marxist or a Muslim will not agree with that of a Christian. The patterning does not evidently arise from a mere inspection of Christian history. Could then those 'ingredients' be the practical living of the Christian life? But this will not do either, since it involves a circularity. The Christian life and Christian faith are part of the same entity; if there is diversity in the one, there is diversity in the other. A patterning cannot arise unless a pattern has already been imposed. Another possibility emerges from the phrase 'the resources which the Christian community makes available'. Could it be that by these 'ingredients' the commission have in mind the Christian tradition as mediated within the worshipping community? This is by far the most likely and promising suggestion, but suffers from a fatal ambiguity. To what worshipping community is the commission referring? Is it all the many different Christian churches, or is it the Anglican church alone? If it is the whole Christian church, then one is simply overwhelmed by the massive diversity of Christian belief and rites, and the claim that some kind of common pattern or method of thinking arises from such 'resources' is plainly falsified by experience. Indeed, if one were honest, the worship of the churches is one of the most deeply rooted and troublesome sources of diversity and disunity. Does the commission not appreciate this, or is it indulging in the rather characteristic Anglican practice of pretending that piety eradicates theological differences? But if it is to the Anglican communion that the commission is referring when it speaks of 'the resources which the Christian community makes available', then at least the diversity is relatively restricted and we have a measure of purchase on the range of Christian experience being invoked. But now, of course, the position becomes rather astonishingly narrow. For if this interpretation of the meaning of the statement is correct what is being said is something as follows: Anglicans find that there is a painful diversity of belief in their midst, but that, arising out of their doctrinal and liturgical traditions there emerges a common pattern or method of thinking which all Anglicans, of whatever persuasion, agree to operate. To operate within the pattern means 'to use in whatever way or proportion integrity allows' the resources which the Anglican communion makes available. But this, one must remark, is not likely to appeal to those Anglicans who find considerable inspiration from the liturgical and theological traditions of denominations other than their own. Moreover, it is to imply something astonishingly optimistic about the sufficiency of the Anglican community to command what one might call the methodological loyalty of its members, especially of its thinking members.

Now it will not escape the attention of the reader that I have subjected some words of the report to a rather close scrutiny, and it will not unfairly be said the reports of this kind do not lend themselves to this kind of analysis. I am prepared to plead guilty to the charge of academic pedantry, however, if it will be allowed me that the substantive issue is an extremely important one. If it is the case that the report has not thought through this matter with sufficient care, then I desire to earn no merit by a merely negative criticism. But the point of substance is nothing less than central to the integrity of the Anglican communion and it is to this that I wish to direct attention.

The question is, what sort of unity binds Anglicans of different persuasions together? It must be said, at once, that of the two relevant sections of the report only one refers explicitly to the situation of contemporary Anglicans. The first, which I have already quoted, speaks generally of the difficulties of diverging beliefs which arise for Christians. Indeed the report as a whole claims that its discussion deals with problems common to all Christians (p. xii). The second passage, however, explicitly speaks of the diversity of attitude towards the creeds within the Church of England. This indeed is only right and proper, since by no means all Christian churches accord to the creeds the position given them in the Anglican church. For Anglicans specifically, then, the report recommends that the diversity of conviction about the creeds be made a creative tension by constant dialogue, determined by three factors; first, by the unceasing effort, aided by every resource of prayer, thought, and common service, to come to a fuller comprehension of the truth; secondly, by a constant reference to the classical tradition of which the scriptures are the foundation and the creeds are part; and, thirdly, by genuine openness to truth from whatever quarter it might come (pp. 38f). From the recital of these three determinants of the dialogue, it looks very much as though we have here a fuller description of what is meant by 'operating within the pattern'. But would not the pattern turn out to be a very different thing indeed if one was supposed to use as a resource not simply the Anglican traditions of worship and doctrine and service (diverse enough as they are), but also those of modern Roman Catholics of all persuasions, of the Orthodox churches, of Pentecostalists and Southern Baptists, of Quakers and Salvationists? That, at least, one must ask; and one must beg leave to doubt whether anything so definite as a common pattern or method of thinking could be claimed as arising from them.

But one further critical remark is called for, before I try to develop some positive counter-proposals. The notion of a pattern of thinking is by no means a novel one in theology or in Anglicanism itself. I propose in a later chapter to examine the suggestion that there exists an Anglican theological method and an independent essay by Paul Wignall at the end of the book outlines four elements of patterns in theology. Of modern writers on theological methodology one can refer to the work of the Roman Catholic writer, Bernard Lonergan, and his *Method in Theology* (1972), as an example of what might be involved in the articulation of 'a normative pattern of operations', relevant to theology. Whatever else the report does or does not achieve it does not, as it claims, *show* that such a pattern exists. Perhaps it does as much as hint that such a pattern might exist, or express the hope that it could be articulated. But of any kind of demonstration it is innocent. *And this innocence is serious*. It is serious, not because one would expect such a report to be capable of producing it, which would, I think, be quite unreasonable. It is serious, rather, because the report seems to have no conception of the fact that it is itself nowhere near producing such a pattern and demonstrating how it operates, and no conception that the Anglican communion seems never to have produced a demonstration of this pattern properly applicable to its contemporary situation. The question, what binds Anglicans together, remains unanswered.

Having found fault with so much of what has been written by Anglicans about Anglicanism, it may have occurred to the reader to ask whether it actually matters that Anglicans are so divided amongst themselves. One might acknowledge that there are certain practical inconveniences in this diversity when one is invited to represent 'the Anglican point of view' in, for example, an ecumenical context. But is it the case in fact that anything very serious is lost in having to admit to a wide range of theological view? Do churches have to stand for particular confessional positions? Or, if other churches, such as the Lutheran or Roman Catholic communions, do have an official stance on central matters, ought the Anglican church necessarily to have one also? Is it not — one hears this frequently said — the peculiar glory of the Church of England that it does not have this kind of doctrinal commitment?

Now it is certainly true that the Anglican reformation lacked the kind of doctrinal definiteness given, for example, to the Lutheran church by Luther and the Lutheran confessional documents; and an explicit part of the seventeenth-century apologia for the Anglican church was that it did not insist on the kind of formulated system of doctrine produced at the Council of Trent. But it would have astonished Cranmer or Hooker to be told that Anglicans had no doctrinal commitment, when the explicit claim which they were making was that the church professed the identical faith of the apostles and of the early church. The point and significance of the Thirty Nine Articles in relation to Anglicanism is also frequently misrepresented. Ambiguous they may be, and related to specific controversies of the sixteenth century. But it is nonsense to say that they are void of doctrinal content, or that they add nothing to the bare confession of the creed. The very reason for omitting in 1865 the phrase from the formula of assent demanding acknowledgment of all and every one of the articles was precisely because this was found to be too restricting to the consciences of nineteenth-century Anglicans. Similarly, the reason for further loosening the terms of the declaration of assent in 1975 was that even the previous ambiguity no longer corresponded to the real divergence of belief which some modern Anglicans professed from the substance of the Articles. In other words, there has taken place a substantial change in the Anglican requirement for doctrinal commitment among its officially commissioned personnel. It is simply not historically correct to suppose that this has always been the case in the Anglican church, or that the present wide doctrinal freedom has always been characteristic of Anglicanism. The case is rather that in response to the pressures initially of controversy and subsequently (and decisively) of biblical and historical criticism, the Anglican church has progressively shed its distinctive confessional commitment, relatively broad though that always was.

But cannot a church manage without a publicly proclaimed doctrinal commitment? This is the real situation which the Church of England faces. Is it not the case that literally anything which any authoritative body or person might one day proclaim to be the doctrinal basis of Anglicanism would be controverted by some notable Anglican the day after? And in this eventuality is it not wiser to live without official stances? 'There are many points which the Church leaves to the discussion of theologians, in that there is no absolute certainty about them', said Pope John, commenting on the distinction between dogmas and open questions. Is not the position in Anglicanism that *everything* is left to the discussion of theologians and that about *nothing* is there thought to be such absolute certainty that it could form the substance of an official proclamation? This seems to be the implication of a statement of Professor Wiles, in his contribution to the essays in *Christian Believing:*

> 'What is important for the Christian community at large is not that it gets its beliefs absolutely clear and definite; it cannot hope to do that if they are really beliefs about God. It is rather that people within the community go on working at the intellectual problems, questioning, testing, developing, and seeking the practical application of the traditions that we have inherited from the past (p. 130).'

Now I believe that there are two responses to this position: First, that, like a lot of liberal thinking, it is parasitic on the positive convictions of those who are clearer and more definite about what they believe; and secondly, that, in fact, the Church of England *has* got definite convictions and insists on a high degree of conformity to them (compared, that is, to some other communions).

To take the first point, it must be said that the Church of England would patently not exist in the form in which it does exist if all its members were as uncertain and unclear about their beliefs as its most liberal members. One cannot imagine such a body insisting on episcopal ordination, or on the celebration of the Eucharist by ordained persons only; one can scarcely imagine it using so controversial a canticle as the

Te Deum or the Gloria; it would, in short, be a very different 'Christian community' indeed. So the references to 'the Christian community' which abound in the writings of liberal theologians need to be examined with some care. For if they refer to the support provided by the church which is actually at present in existence, then it must be acknowledged how substantially dependent that community is upon groups with positive convictions on the very matters which liberals find so doubtful. This is not an unfamiliar situation. Those who question a received tradition are quite frequently not wholly convinced of the certainty of their own beliefs. Sometimes, indeed, they find it very difficult to achieve a thorough articulation of their positive convictions. What they are sure about is that there is a subject to be discussed. If the tradition can vindicate itself it will do so in due course; if the tradition is merely enforced by assertion and repression, the objections will be raised with renewed vigour. There is thus nothing anomalous in a situation in which a body both insists that it has a definite teaching, and also is tolerant of a free discussion of that teaching.

The second answer to the question whether a church can live without a publicly proclaimed doctrinal commitment is that, in fact, the Church of England has a substantial and quite vigorously enforced discipline, though not so much in the direct area of church doctrine as in the indirect area of canon law and liturgical order. This is a substantial point and needs to be carefully expounded; to this end I wish to make a number of subsidiary points.

1. All our previous discussion of the party situation in the Church of England has tended to show that there is within it a substantial quantity of contradictory opinion and conviction on major doctrinal matters. The various techniques employed by Anglican apologists to disguise the situation have been finally shown to be bankrupt. We have reached the point where the question raised in the 1948 Lambeth Report as to the coherence of the Anglican communion needs to be faced with new urgency. The integrity of the communion is in question, because it appears to be offering the propositions of the Christian gospel as topics for debate and discussion, rather than to be witnessing to the mighty act of God in Christ.

However, all the examples we have discussed hitherto have derived from doctrinal controversies, or attempts to interpret them, and from the content of declarations of assent required of ordained and other ministers in the Church of England. Nothing has yet been said about its liturgical life. But in the 1975 Declaration of Assent quoted above the promise is given by the candidate that in public prayer and administration of the sacraments he will use only the forms of service which are authorised or allowed by canon. This, together with the oath of canonical obedience sworn to the bishop of the diocese, and all the other provisions of canon law relating to the conduct of public worship, the administration of the sacraments, the furnishing of churches and the dress of ministers (save for the purposes of recreation and other justifiable reasons!), provide a substantially regulated framework for the actual life of the Anglican community.

2. It is of course true that there is a long tradition of illegality in the liturgical life of the Church of England. It is interesting to recall, that at the precise moment when Charles Gore was seeking to arouse the Church authorities to take legal action against the modern churchmen for their heretical Christ-ology, he felt constrained to admit publicly that it was anglo-catholics who had to bear part of the blame for the collapse of corporate discipline within the church.[2] In this respect the Church of England is quite probably the least law-abiding of the provinces of the Anglican communion, so that to assume that canon law is a dead letter in Anglicanism may well be a piece of English provincialism. It must be frankly said that the 100 years of gross contempt for canon law was the most serious price paid for the party conflicts of the nineteenth century. From 1928, when Parliament refused to authorise the Revised Prayer Book, until the passing of the Alternative and Other Services Measure of 1965 which made it lawful for the Church to use experi-mental services, the Church of England seemed to be drifting towards a kind of congregationalism, with numerous parishes devising their own liturgies for themselves. It is certainly true that the diversity is hardly less in the present period of experi-mental rites, each of which incorporates a variety of optional and alternative features. But there is some significance in the fact that this diversity is now largely contained within prescribed limits, and is subject to proper canonical authority, hard though it may be to enforce.

3. Now it is obviously the case that the worship of the

church, as prescribed in particular verbal forms, has some doctrinal content. The collects and other prayers, the canticles and the responses both contain and imply particular doctrines. None of these, of course demand from the worshipper the same kind of assent implied in the saying of the creed. Indeed not even the creed, in its context in worship, necessarily implies that one who utters it has a conscious and definite knowledge of, and assents to, the implications of each and every clause. Still more so the prayers, where the worshipper is free to use them as vehicles for his own devotion, while drawing support from the common use of them by Christians of many different styles and even convictions. Nonetheless, the prayers contain, express and imply particular Christian doctrines and are strongly influenced by the positive doctrinal beliefs of earlier generations. A tremendous weight is borne by these common liturgical forms in an age when the direct declaration of belief has been substantially minimised.

4. But it is not merely the case that certain doctrines are referred to directly or indirectly in the words of the church's services, it is also the case that the whole ethos of the church has a doctrinal basis and doctrinal implications. By participating in a liturgy a Christian exposes himself to a number of doctrinal influences, of which he may not be directly aware. When he hears the Scriptures read in a service, he will, of course, hear what the passage teaches. But he may not be consciously aware that the very fact *that* the scripture has been read expresses a doctrine. This example can be pursued still further. If a church adopts the practice of selecting special portions of scripture for public reading (the anthology principle), that expresses one sort of doctrine about scripture. If it maintains the ancient Anglican practice of reading the whole of scripture from Genesis to Revelation, that expresses another doctrine. Similar points may be made about almost every aspect of what is sung, said or done in church. Anglicans (or, at least, members of the Church of England), with their astonishing capacity to take these things for granted, forget that most forms of Anglican practice, from the use of set forms of prayer to the vesting of the officiant at divine service, were once highly controversial and had to be justified at great pains against rival views. If not so controversial today, and if not indeed so important in the minds of those who participate in liturgies with a free-wheeling tolerance of

traditional usage far removed from the fierce partisanships of the past, nonetheless it is the case not merely that liturgy expresses doctrines, but the *performance* of liturgy expresses doctrines. And in the Anglican church many aspects of the performance of a liturgy are subject to regulation by canon law.

5. The argument of the last two points is intended to establish the fact that the present Anglican church has incorporated a regulated doctrinal structure in the content of its liturgy, and in the rules governing its public performance. This is not to be interpreted, however, as a way of smuggling in a uniform confessional stance by the back door. It must be admitted, as mentioned above, that the words of prayers are not assented to as the words of credal declarations. The worshipper is free to interpret them as he wishes, and to use any part and neglect any part without restraint. Moreover, in the multiplicity of modern service books (within the Church of England, let alone the whole Anglican communion) there is great variety, including some doctrinal variety. Also it must be admitted that the performance of the liturgy, while subject to regulation, is still astonishingly various. Thus there is a considerable contrast of styles to be seen, corresponding, it may be, to a different conception of worship, between a traditionally formal Prayer Book service, and a modern informal liturgy. All this is true, and greatly qualifies any sense in which Anglicans can claim a basic unity.

6. And there is a further point to be made, which introduces another sort of complexity, namely the difficulty about any precision in the interpretation of practices. It is extremely easy to make mistakes about the motivation of actions; and it is no less easy to find a variety of meanings in the rituals and practices of the church. Even where certain rituals are said to have a particular significance, other motivations can sometimes be found for them. The interpretation of practices is rarely exhaustive, and may sometimes be very inexact. With the reintroduction of certain mediaeval practices into the nineteenth-century Church of England, there came a number of rather bogus explanations, some of which are still repeated as their rationale.

What this all amounts to is a warning against supposing that the mere fact that certain things are prescribed, for example, that the holy table shall be covered at the time of divine service 'with a covering of silk or other decent stuff' (Canon F2), has one particular significance. The fact that this canon refers to 'the holy table' rather than to 'the altar' is, or at least was, highly significant. The fact that there is a canon regulating the practice is certainly significant and provides one reason why Anglican churches do not look like Baptist chapels. But Anglicans persist in a great variety of practices and attitudes regarding the covering of the table or altar, and any attempt to propose a single rationale would falsify the situation. There is no question of a uniform confessional stance arising out of such regulations; the most that can be claimed is that arising out of the observance of such regulations, as out of the use of prescribed forms of liturgy, certain particular ways of approach to Christian discipleship are constantly reinforced. And it is this, if anything, which gives coherence to the Anglican communion.

The importance of a liturgy backed by canon law is a widely recognised feature of Anglicanism, most recently observed in a work entitled *Anglican Vision* (1971) by Dr. de Mendieta. The author, a former Roman Catholic Benedictine monk, asking by what positive bond the Anglican communion is held together, wrote: 'The answer probably lies in the field of their public and common worship, rather than of explicit and clearly defined dogma.'[3] This bond consists nowadays not just of the Prayer Book of 1662, but the more complex and diverse unity of the liturgies which have, in the course of time, sprung from it. Dr. de Mendieta added three further elements to this bond, the consciousness of continuity with the mediaeval and early church, the principle of compromise employed in official church documents and the emphasis on spiritual freedom, each of which, one may comment, are principally characteristics of its liturgical life and of its canon law.

We cannot, however, leave the matter here. The point of attempting to articulate that for which the Anglican communion stands is not merely to identify what is specifically Anglican; it is, rather, to subject what is said to be specifically Anglican to criticism.

Criticism is essential to the health of a church. Friedrich Schleiermacher, perhaps the most powerful modern exponent of the church's need of criticism, proposed a special discipline in theology, which he called 'polemics', especially devoted to the discernment of 'diseased deviations' creeping into the church's life. The church, he argued, was indelibly stamped with the polemical circumstances of its own origins, the criticism by Jesus of Pharisaic Judaism. Ever since then Christianity has demonstrated an ineradicable restlessness with its own inner life, which, since the reformation, has been powerfully reinforced by the discovery of the true extent of the possibility of spiritual decline. The implication of the doctrine that the church must ever be ready to reform itself is that no church is immune from the insidious processes of adaptation to an environment. Nor is a church which claims never to have changed in better case, since meanings change even when practices or words remain identical. If the Christian church proposes faithfully to preach the gospel, it has no alternative but to launch out into the ambiguities of interaction with its environment, an interaction in which it must keep itself open to criticism, and be ready to change its ways.

This preparedness for criticism and openness to change is vital in the light of the seriousness of what it is doing, which is nothing less than providing an educational matrix for the nurture of Christian character. *Every* aspect of church life is involved in this educative process, doctrines and liturgies, ceremonial, architecture, and ancillary services. Each of these express in one way or another aspects of how that church believes Christians may grow in their faith. The music of the church may be taken as an example. Recurrently in the history of the church it was found necessary for church authority to issue regulations concerning styles and length of music in church services. Clearly it was considered that music had a particular function in worship not identical with its function outside worship. Clearly it was also felt possible for the practice of the church to get progressively out of balance and to need correction, if it was not to serve as a distraction from the worship. This could not be a matter for once-for-all decision, since musical styles and taste are subject to change. The positive aspect of the use of music, its contribution in the specific context of worship to the lifting up of heart and mind to God, is to be dominant. And that, in today's disastrously divided cultural world, is an acutely difficult matter of wisdom and judgement, requiring at once respect for traditional standards and sensitivity towards the danger of turning the Church into a cultured ghetto.

The place of music in worship is, however, only one example. The person who worships in a church Sunday by Sunday is someone whose attitudes towards the practice of Christian worship are being formed in a particular way. And the question is, is that way true to the aims of Christian discipleship, true to the effective carrying out of the will of God in the present? It need not be so. It may be the case that the ethos of the church, running through things as diverse as the robing of the minister, the intelligibility or otherwise of the prayers, and the position accorded to the laity suggest strongly that religion was something performed on Sundays by the minister, which it was vital to witness but had no direct bearing on daily life. Important changes have been effected by observation of the unsatisfactoriness of certain proceedings, for example the practice of holding baptisms totally separated from the life of the congregation. The business of providing an educational matrix for the nurture of Christian character is too important a matter for a complacent attitude towards one's traditional ways of doing things. Even long and valued traditions — valued, that is, by those parts of the community well adapted to them — may come to have a radically alienating effect on a still larger section. This, too, is a matter for criticism, argument and mature judgement, not a matter for a poll of public opinion and still less for following the dictates of personal preference.

What, therefore, I wish to recommend is that it is the Anglican community's responsibility to articulate the characteristics of the matrix it provides for the growth of Christian character, and to subject that self-understanding to criticism. Institutions, one may safely say, are not wholly successful in the task of self-identification, and one must not look for such writing in the Reports of the Lambeth Conferences. Self-portraiture presents an irresistible opportunity for the insidiously deep processes of self-deception and the temptations of selective blindness. It is difficult enough for individuals to raise to conscious articulation the major aspects of their instinctual life. And what is here proposed is that an institution set itself the task of recognising that which is by now deeply instinctive in its liturgical life and canon law. To use the metaphor of 'an instinctual life' is not wholly inappropriate in the light of the temptations spoken of above. But difficult though I acknowledge the task to be, the right question to ask is, what in fact is the alternative? The alternative is to continue to implement an implicit set of commitments, by which the lives of the membership of the Church are shaped and nurtured, without any assurance that these commitments are in fulfilment of the imperatives of the gospel. It is to permit the Church unconsciously to adopt features and assumptions imposed by the general cultural life of the community in which it operates.

The doctrine of the guidance of the Holy Spirit, which is not infrequently introduced at this point, does not help us. Indeed it is that Church — the Roman Church — which expressly believes that the Holy Spirit is directly operative in its decisions, which most rigorously attempts to conform all its practice to a carefully cultivated understanding of the church. The appeals to the doctrine of the guidance of the Holy Spirit which are made by modern Anglican apologists for what one can only call institutional drift, are the very opposite of a vigorous and intellectually disciplined inquiry into the nature of the relationship of Anglicanism to the universal Church of Christ.

The conclusion, then, of this stage of my book is as follows: the Anglican church, which has developed, under the impact of modern liberal theology, a breadth of doctrinal tolerance of doubt and internal contradiction unparalleled by that of other episcopal churches, has an urgent responsibility to articulate what it stands for as an institution in its liturgy and canon law, and to subject that content to rigorous criticism. This process will in the first instance reveal the incontrovertible fact that there exist doctrines repeatedly affirmed by all parts of its liturgical tradition, including its most modern additions. The doctrine of the incarnation is the most obvious of these; indeed one could argue that the incarnation is the basis of dogma in the Anglican church, provided that by 'dogma' one understood not what the church had defined but more generally that for which it publicly stood. This, however, would only be the first stage in the process of articulation, important though it would be in some quarters to establish the fact that the Anglican church had a standpoint. The next stage would be to elucidate how this standpoint was interpreted by the toleration extended to its overt critics, and by the fact that the standpoint is primarily communicated in the context of worship. The arguments which now rage about the meaning and status of the idea of incarnation are rightly regarded as fundamental; but they are very far from being completely satisfactory in their treatment of how the doctrine functions, at least for Anglicans. Briefly it can be put like this: Anyone can observe that the doctrine of the incarnation is basic to Anglican liturgical life as enforced by canon law. Almost anyone can, on the strength of a little theological education, write essays attacking or defending it. But it takes real theological skill to see how this doctrine both underlies and is interpreted by a worshipping body at once tolerant of theological criticism of it and yet aware of the responsibility as a matrix for the nurture of Christian character. The question is, what does the Anglican church do to ensure that such skill is fostered?

FOOTNOTES

1. This is part of the description given of one of the approaches to Christian believing given considerable prominence in the Report (on pp. 7-11 and 36-7) and nowhere stated to be incompatible with membership or ordained ministry in the Church.
2. See G. L. Prestige, *Charles Gore*, p. 456
3. E. A. de Mendieta, *Anglican Vision* (London, 1971), p. 56

Chapter 4

DOES 'ANGLICAN THEOLOGY' EXIST?

THE kind of self-understanding which, I have been arguing, is required in the modern Anglican church, indeed which is required in any church, should form an integral part of the study by members of that communion of ecclesiology, the doctrine of the church. When we think of the contents of ecclesiology, we may very well think of the first instance of traditional topics such as the authority of Christ and the authority of the church, ministry and ordained ministry, the sacraments and sacramental grace. But there are other matters which also belong to ecclesiology. For this subject area of theology includes not merely what is said or implied by way of eucharistic theology in an order of service of Holy Communion, but also the fact that what is said is (or may be) capable of different interpretations, or the fact that there is not just one order, but several alternative orders. For a church may hold such a view of itself that it feels obliged to insist on one uniform doctrine of the eucharist expressed in highly precise language, reinforced by particular rubrics of clear significance. That would imply one sort of ecclesiology. On the other hand a church may consider it quite consistent with its understanding of itself and its mission not to be precise in its liturgical formulations, and even deliberately to cultivate ambiguous or balanced language. Further it may feel that nothing important is lost if there is not just one eucharistic rite, but several, and if representatives of the congregation itself are instructed to join with the priest in choosing the liturgy which seems to them the most appropriate in the circumstances. And that, surely, reflects a very different understanding of what the church *is*.

This, I fear, is a much neglected point in Anglican ecclesiology, which, weak as it is, tends to concentrate on the more obviously central questions, such as the 'notes' of the church (its unity, holiness, apostolicity and catholicity). These, it is thought, are the major questions of ecclesiology, together with the doctrines of the ministry and sacraments. Other questions, for example, matters of ceremonial, are swept aside in a traditional Anglican phrase, as matters of indifference. The mistake of this gesture is not in designating them as indifferent, but in failing to realise that the designation is itself significant of a particular view of the nature and function of the church. In particular, to take the matter no further, it signifies that nothing essential is threatened by a relative degree of diversity of liturgical use and practice. What is further signified may very well be controversial. Does, for example, it suggest that Anglicans set a very low priority on visible unity? Is it the case that Anglicans expect there always to be congregations in the same town practically unable to come together in worship because one interprets the freedom given by the Anglican structure in one way, and another in a radically different way? (In such circumstances Anglicans of one group or another have frequently found it easier to co-operate with the congregation of another denomination than with their fellow Anglicans). Or is it the case that Anglicans set such a very high store on the structures of their own church, on the place of bishops and the role of synodical government, that they are prepared to go to almost any lengths of toleration of internal conflict and diversity of style in order to prevent schism? One could argue with greater or lesser cogency for either of these positions, and in both there would be considerable implications for the doctrine of the church. But the point particularly to notice is that either of the positions, if rigorously pursued, has a very important bearing on the contribution which the Anglican church ought to be making to the ecumenical movement. Anglican theologians ought, I would argue, to be developing an understanding of the sense in which the present Anglican communion is 'part of', or participates in, the universal Church of Christ. They have done so in the past, but, if the argument of the previous sections is correct, their depiction of the actual state of the Anglican communion was vitiated by the prevalence of certain myths about the nature of Anglicanism. There is now a need to perform the task again with a new sense of realism and determination.

But is there 'an Anglican contribution'? In answering this question we turn to a problem which has continually hung about the whole discussion hitherto without being explicitly acknowledged. Is there such a thing as Anglican theology? In conversation with my colleagues in the Anglican communion I find a very ready acceptance for the firm denial of such a proposal. I have already referred to the denial that Anglicans have a particular doctrinal position to defend in the sense in which, say, Lutherans may feel obliged to defend Luther's theology or the Lutheran confessional documents, and this denial I shall discuss in the chapter which follows. What we are asking here is a somewhat different question, namely whether Anglican theologians, when they write theology, write, consciously or unconsciously, Anglican theology. Of course, if there are no Anglican confessional documents and no classical Anglican theologian or theologians, then the Anglican character of a theology written by Anglicans will, if it exists at all, be a more difficult thing to detect. But the disinclination to believe in the existence of Anglican theology is a deeply implanted notion, which cuts at the root of the position which I am advocating. For if there is no Anglican theology, developed out of the distinctively Anglican commitments embodied both in what is regulated and is left unregulated in its liturgy and canon law, then there is little point in pleading for a renewed Anglican self-understanding as a preliminary to a new attack on the question of the contribution of Anglicanism to ecumenism. Fortunately, however, I believe it is possible to show that the assertion that there is no Anglican theology is based on a series of misunderstandings.

Let us take one influential statement of the position I hope to refute. It occurs in William Temple's Introduction to the Report on Doctrine in the Church of England, where he wrote:

> 'If this Report is to render the service for which it is designed, the purpose and method of its composition must be borne in mind. As we have already indicated, it is in no sense the outline of a systematic theology; that is something in one way more, but in another less, ambitious than what we have attempted. For a systematic theology proceeds from premises regarded as assured, and from these builds up a fabric by continuous reasoning. There are systems of Catholic theology and of Protestant theology. To them we have, or course, owed much. But there is not, and the majority of us do not desire that there should be, a system of distinctively Anglican theology. The Anglican Churches have received and hold the faith of Catholic Christendom, but they have exhibited a rich variety in methods both of approach and interpretation. (p.25).'

In this statement a number of things are confused with each other, whose separation helps us see more clearly not merely the possibility of, but actually the necessity for Anglican theology.

1. First of all there is the statement that the report does not set out to be a systematic theology. This is perfectly intelligible, though not precisely for the reasons which seem to be implied. It is said, for example, that the report is not for expert theologians and avoids technical terms; which is true enough, but does not thereby disqualify it from being systematic. It is said, also, that the aim of the report is 'to promote unity and mutual appreciation within the Church of England, partly by the interpretation of one school of thought to another, and partly by pointing to the fulness of a truth diversely apprehended in different quarters' (p. 25). These two activities are quite separate from each other and neither is inconsistent with systematic theology. The activity of interpreting divergent schools of thought to each other is, of course, something quite different from systematic theology; and the report certainly on occasions produces descriptions of different points of view and suggestions regarding the point at which these may be in agreement. Nothing, however, would prevent this activity from being a prolegomenon to systematics. Moreover the other task of 'pointing to the fulness of truth diversely apprehended in different quarters' could be taken to require nothing less than a properly articulated systematic theology, in which 'the fulness of truth diversely apprehended' comes to expression. This phrase of truly Mauricean obscurity suggests at once a strictly limited objective ('pointing to') and an extraordinarily ambitious objective ('fulness of truth'). In fact the report can be more accurately described. It follows a traditional enough pattern of doctrinal topics, starting with the sources and authority of doctrine, and moving through God and redemption, church and sacraments, and eschatology. Internally the report varies between straight expositions of Christian doctrine in the manner of a catechetical handbook, presumably on matters where there was no internal disagreement between the members of the commission, and reports of differing views, sometimes among the members of the commission, sometimes in the Anglican church as a whole. In the latter case an attempt is usually made to find an agreed statement at an acceptable level of ambiguity, sometimes relating the divergences to earlier controversies in the church. The reason, however, why the report is not systematic is because

none of the philosophical conditions of a systematic theology are fulfilled. There is no attempt at epistemology or theory of knowledge; there is no discussion of ontology; there is little attempt to create a uniform vocabulary (technical or non-technical) — in short, no one who had a clear idea of the style and content of a systematic theology would be able to confuse the report with one for a moment.

2. 'Systematic theology', Temple states, 'proceeds from premises regarded as assured' — he then speaks of there being systems of catholic and of protestant theology. This too seems to contain a confusion of Mauricean origin. The *systematic* character of any systematic theology derives from a massive attempt at consistency in reasoning, an attempt whose seriousness can be gauged either by sophistication of its philosophical equipment or by relation of each and every feature of the doctrinal structure to a fundamental understanding of divine revelation. If there have been 'systems' of Roman Catholic and protestant theology, it is because there have been individual Roman Catholics and protestants who have essayed this massive task, for example, Thomas Aquinas and (to my mind, with less certain a claim to be so regarded) John Calvin. It would, however, be a matter of very great difficulty to state what the 'assured premises' of either of their systems were, from which the fabric of their theology was supposedly built up by a process of continuous reasoning; and such a statement would almost certainly give rise to scholarly controversy. Temple's idea of systematic theology seems, therefore, to be seriously defective. Indeed, not unlike Maurice, he seems to imply that the attempt to be intellectually consistent is a kind of defect in a theology. But the confusion here is between systematic theology *per se*, and what may be spoken of, in a rough and ready way, as 'the Catholic system'. The latter is better spoken of as a corpus of dogma. Whether one can speak thus of 'the protestant system' may certainly be doubted, and the reason is instructive. Wheareas there are numerous different protestant systems, such as those of Calvin, Luther, Melanchthon and the other protestant dogmaticians (of very varying degrees of intellectual sophistication), of none of them is it true that they have achieved the degree of authority attained by Thomism in the modern Roman Catholic church. Before Thomas it might have been possible to speak of the Catholic corpus of dogma; but not of

'the Catholic system'. But church dogma is not the same thing as systematic theology; one has only to consider the work of a modern protestant systematic theologian, Paul Tillich, to realise that by no stretch of the imagination does the articulation of a system imply acceptance of dogma.

3. Temple states that the majority of the commission 'do not desire that there should be a system of distinctive Anglican theology'. It is interesting to note that in 1925, E. G. Selwyn, one of the commission's members, had published an essay entitled, 'Anglican Theology and English Religion'[1], where an attempt of some interest was made to speak of 'the distinctive witness of Anglican theology'. That notwithstanding, Temple's confident expression of the commission's desire is characteristic-ally ambiguous and confused. It might mean, for instance, that the members of the commission had no desire to see one single system of distinctively Anglican theology. This may indeed be granted; but then, of course, the earlier reference to systems of Roman Catholic and of protestant theology cease to be intel-ligible. Who could be said to have produced the single system of distinctively protestant theology, for example, before, let alone after, the enlightenment? The fact that one could not produce an agreed systematisation of Anglicanism does not in any way differentiate Anglicanism from modern (or even sixteenth-century) protestantism. If that was Temple's and the com-mission's meaning then they are guilty of absurd misrepresent-ation.

Perhaps, then, this statement may mean that there should exist nothing claiming to be 'distinctively Anglican', since Anglicans have no other desire than to be catholic. Any theo-logian who happened to be an Anglican would not describe his own work as Anglican, but as catholic theology. This seems to be stated in the sentence, 'the Anglican Churches have received and hold the faith of Catholic Christendom' (though in the clause that follows there is a confusing reversion to the theme of Anglican diversity). Let us examine, then, the suggestion that Anglican theology is simply catholic theology. Perhaps what is being said is that *only* Anglican, and not any other kind of theology, has the right to be called catholic theology, because only Anglicans hold the true faith. This position is absurdly arrogant and so manifestly at variance with the repeatedly state ' view of Anglicans that they do not deny the possession of the catholic faith to other orthodox denominations, that it does not seem to need examination. The only alternative, then, is to suppose that Temple means that Anglicans believe that their theology is catholic (though not in any exclusive sense). But it has to be faced that Anglicans are not the only ones to *claim* that their theology is catholic. Scarcely any informed Christian would do less. No Roman Catholic would regard his theology as less catholic because it is Roman, or Greek Orthodox his theology less orthodox because it is characteristic of the Greek Church, or Lutheran or Calvinist less wholly true because it is protestant. The designations 'Roman, 'Greek' and 'Protestant' are verbal conventions useful for identifying the differing features of various accounts of Christian faith, not alternatives to the term 'catholic'. And why should we not, in the same sense, speak of Anglican theology as both catholic *and* distinctively Anglican? Why should Anglicans be shy of actually having something identifiable in their approach to the truth of the Christian faith? Once it becomes obvious that there is no one Anglican systematic theology, any more than there is one Lutheran or Calvinist, one Greek Orthodox, or even one Roman Catholic, then nothing is lost if non-Anglicans discover that Anglicans do, as a matter of fact, bring a rather distinctive approach or group of approaches to questions of theological discussion.

The situation is, in fact, a little comic. In ecumenical circles Anglicans fall over backwards in their attempts to deny that they are speaking for the official party line of their own communion. And precisely by doing so, they identify themselves as characteristically Anglican. Englishmen, Hume once said, have no distinguishing characteristics, unless that be the very characteristic which distinguishes them.

What we have seen in this examination of Temple's denial of the desirability of a system of distinctively Anglican theology is a confusion of a number of separate matters, which can be briefly summarized as follows:

1. The fact that, relatively speaking, Anglicans lack a sharply outlined corpus of doctrines embodied in the work of a reformer or in confessional documents.

2. The fact that Anglicans have set a high premium on spiritual freedom, which makes its central authorities reluctant to lay down official guidelines or to discipline heretics.

3. The fact that Anglicans frequently claim to hold the faith of the catholic church, meaning by this, usually, the faith of the undivided church.

4. The fact that no theology is sufficiently identified by any secondary descriptive term, such as Roman, Greek or Anglican, and that of all these theologies the only important claim is that it should be true.

This last point deserves to be developed. It should be obvious that all theology must claim, if it is to be Christian theology, that it is true. And the criteria for the truth of a Christian theology are identical for the criteria by which a church criticises its own self-understanding. That is to say, it could not be a satisfactory position that such-and-such was the way Anglicans believed the Christian church should live, and that the same view was theologically untrue. If there is any way for an Anglican to identify what his church stands for as a communion, as I have argued, then it must be the case that that understanding is either consistent or inconsistent with the Christian gospel. If it is inconsistent, or partly inconsistent, then that Anglican knows that he must set out to criticise and reform his own church to make it consistent; if he believes it is consistent then what he has developed may be properly spoken of as Anglican theology of the church at one and the same time as catholic, and characteristically Anglican. There is no third possibility. Indeed it strikes one as a little absurd to have to argue with such pedantry for so obvious a point.

Why then, are Anglicans so paralysed by the thought they might have to formulate and defend a doctrine of the church for their own communion in the service of the universal Church? Partly, it may be, out of a very proper humility. On the face of it, it seems very unlikely indeed that any insight of universal significance emerges out of the unpromising circumstances of the Henrician reformation. But that is one possibility, perhaps no more surprising than the familiar claims made for the outcome of events at other particular times and places. But there seems to be another side to the situation. English Anglicans have been mesmerised by the false idea that their ecclesiastical arrangements are of a purely practical character, and neither have, nor require, any merely theoretical justification. And this proposal, it must be said, is the very reverse of humble. It rests on a view of the nature of English society and of an occult entity known as 'the English mind' whose roots lie no deeper than the Industrial Revolution and the period of colonial expansion, when the nation learnt to pride itself on its technological inventions and success in trade, and to despise the philosophical achievements of a generation of foreign thinkers, largely of German origin. This poisonous arrogance, of course, cloaks itself in more acceptable dress in academic company. The fact that F. D. Maurice knew little German did not prevent him from formulating a general theory of how English and German theology began at opposite poles from each other, the English from what is above and addresses us, the German from what is below and seeks for an object beyond itself.[2] (It testifies to the intellectual poverty of all such generalisations that precisely the opposite contrast was alleged to exist by Karl Barth one hundred years later at the Amsterdam Assembly of the World Council of Churches). Even those who did not descend to attack what, in the nineteenth century, was offensively called 'Germanism' were sometimes happy to avail themselves of the popular idea that the Anglo-Saxon, in some ineffable way, penetrated to the heart of things without actually being so vulgar as to show how he did it. Characteristic is the *bon mot* of the Scots Presbyterian scholar, H. R. Mackintosh: 'the Anglo-Saxon mind on the average has considerably less learning; but very often, I think, it exhibits a much sounder judgement.'[3]

No merely rational arguments can hope to be victorious over such impermeable confidence. English Anglicans must just hope to be rescued from it by Anglicans of other racial origins. But at the very least certain remarks can be made. The Anglican theologian does not need to be oppressed by the example of the diligence of German protestant scholarship; he may take his lessons elsewhere, from the example of French Roman Catholic theology, for intance, or from the very substantial contributions to theology now emanating from America, both Catholic and protestant. Might it not be the case that Anglican theologians have for too long been complacent and lazy, and that their reluctance to formulate and defend Anglican theology is a serious disservice not only to their own communion, but also to the universal Church of Christ? Such a view is at least conceivable when we examine the sad state of Anglican theology today.

FOOTNOTES

1. In E. G. Selwyn, *The Approach to Christianity* (London, 1925), pp. 236-279
2. In a letter to a pupil, written in 1848, quoted in F. Maurice, *The Life of Frederick Denison Maurice,* Vol 1 (London, 1884), p. 468
3. *Types of Modern Theology* (London, 1937), p. 4

Chapter 5

DOES 'ANGLICAN METHOD' EXIST?

BUT there is a further claim which it is appropriate to examine at this point, namely that, whether or not there is a specifically Anglican dogmatic theology, there is a specifically Anglican theological method. Writing on the question, 'What is Anglican Theology?', the then Van Mildert Professor of Divinity in the University of Durham, Arthur Michael Ramsey, stated in 1945:

> 'There is such a thing as Anglican theology and it is sorely needed at the present day. But because it is neither a system nor a confession (the idea of an Anglican 'confessionalism' suggests something that never has been and never can be) but a method, a use and a direction, it cannot be defined or even percieved as a 'thing in itself', and it may elude the eyes of those who ask 'What is it?' and 'Where is it?' It has been proved, and will be proved again, by its fruit and its works.'[1]

This method he finds instanced in Hooker and in F. D. Maurice, and consists in a particular way in which scripture, tradition and reason are combined as authorities for Christian doctrine. Contemporary Anglicanism needs, he holds, to rediscover itself, not by taking over a revived neo-Thomism or a form of Barthianism. Rather it needs to follow, in a mode appropriate to the twentieth century, the same method as was operated in the sixteenth. The appeal to scripture must recognise the work of critical scholars; the reference to tradition cannot be content with a static appeal to the undivided church, but must be an appeal to the Christian experience of creed, sacrament, order and liturgy; and the role of reason is to be found both in its distinctive use of scripture and tradition, and in the Anglican insistence on not endowing proper authority with the accolade of infallibility. He concludes:

> 'In these tasks the Anglican will not suppose that he has a system or a confession that can be defined and commended side by side with those of others: indeed the use of the word 'Anglicanism' can be very misleading. Rather will he claim that his tasks look beyond 'isms' to the Gospel of God and to the Catholic Church which he tries to serve with a method, use and direction needed as greatly today as in the past. *Loquere filiis Israel ut profiscantur* (p.6).'

I have already commented on what I believe to be the impossibility of supposing that Anglicans alone of all the communions of Christendom manage to escape designation by a term ending in '-ism'. The interesting question which this position raises is whether or not one can have a distinctive theological method without having a distinctive theological content. In this connection one might remark on one feature of Ramsey's essay, which concerns his identification of the role of the doctrine of the incarnation in Anglicanism. Among the illustrations of the Anglican 'use' which he cites are 'modern works which expound the incarnation in its relation to the evolution of man and nature while fully conserving its unique, redemptive and transcendental character' (p.3). Furthermore one of the reasons he gives for Anglicans being justified in not being at home 'with the divinity broadly and somewhat incorrectly called Barthian' is 'the loosening of the neo-Calvinists' hold upon the incarnation as a central principle'. He continues:

> 'Partly this is seen in a failure to make that estimate of Man which the Incarnation demands. Partly this is seen in a readiness (observable in different degrees in some writers) to part with the idea of the Incarnation itself, since if all that is needed is 'an irruption into history for man's salvation' there is no special importance in the doctrine of God made Man.' (p.5)

Controversial though it would be to apply these strictures either to Brunner (whose *The Mediator* was published in English with an enthusiastic Foreword by J. K. Mozley in 1934) or to Barth (whose *Church Dogmatics* 1/2 had appeared in 1938), the point to be made is that the remarks are obviously of substantial, not methodological, import. If it is the case that Anglicans so value the doctrine of incarnation that they use it as a criterion for distinguishing their theology from that of others, then Anglican divinity is committed not merely to a *method*, but also to a particular doctrinal content. And although this commitment may not distinguish Anglicans from all other Christian denominations, it is certainly *one* of the things which distinguishes them from some.

Another exponent of the view that Anglicanism is not a theological system but a particular method is McAdoo, whose survey of Anglican theological method in the seventeenth century must certainly rank as one of the most significant contributions to Anglican scholarship in the last twenty years.[2] In the preface McAdoo says that his purpose in writing the book is to show, by reference to the writings of Anglicans in the seventeenth century, that the absence of what he terms 'an official theology in Anglicanism' is something deliberate, 'for it has always regarded the teaching and practice of the un- divided church of the first five centuries as a criterion.' This adhesian to 'undifferentiated catholicism' was accompanied by liberality of outlook on secondary matters, a combination of stances found subsequently in Gore's championing of 'liberal catholicism'. From the seventeenth century to the present, it can be seen (according to this view) that 'the distinctiveness of Anglicanism proceeds not from a systematic theology but from the spirit in which theological questions are handled' (p.v.) Specifically this consists in the appeal to scripture, to antiquity and to reason conjointly.

> 'Seventeenth-century Anglicanism, taking it by and large, saw no solution to the problem of authority which did not admit of the mutually illuminating relationship of scripture, antiquity and reason, and refused any solution which insu- lated authority against the testing of history and the free action of reason. It must be such an authority as can stand investigation and command freely-given adherence. It must evoke rather than repress the response of the individual, and refuse to pronounce on matters that are not essential ' (p.410).

McAdoo then follows this passage with illustrations of Gore's attitude towards authority which are in agreement with the above.

When we ask ourselves the same question we addressed to Michael Ramsey's proposals, namely whether or not there is commitment in this position to a particular doctrinal content as well as a particular method, the answer must surely be that there is. In the case of Gore we can see this fact perfectly clearly. As we have shown, when the modernists 'reinterpreted' the doctrine of the incarnation Gore accused them (especially Rashdall) of heresy. In commenting on this episode Ramsey offers the view that the Report on Doctrine in the Church of England implicitly rejects Rashdall's and Bethune-Baker's christology. Gore, he believes, had been right in his diagnosis of a doctrine which was radically different from the historic faith concerning the God and man.

> 'While in the treatment of the Incarnation in the Report it is allowed that it is legitimate to approach the doctrine from either the Alexandrine or the Antiochene standpoints or

> their modern equivalents, there is within this comprehensive *speculum* of contemporary Anglican teaching no place whatever for that view of deity and manhood which in the hands of Rashdall and Bethune-Baker had loomed so large in the Modernism of two decades earlier.'[3]

Whether this view of the report is right or wrong, it substantially illustrates one point, namely that in Gore's mind commitment to historic faith implied commitment to a particular doctrinal content. Again it is irrelevant that other churches also have such a commitment, and that Anglicanism is not *sufficiently* identified by this fact on its own. There is a distinction between a *necessary* and a *sufficient* condition; and Gore's position was quite simply that it is a necessary condition of membership of the Anglican church that one assent to the doctrine of the incarnation as confessed in the historic creeds. Those who did not so assent could not be included within the understanding of Anglican comprehensiveness, because Anglicanism implied acceptance of this doctrine as distinct from what he felt to be the barely disguised unitarianism of Rashdall.

We see, then, that Gore himself would have quite unhesitatingly affirmed particular content as consequential upon the operation of the method he espoused. And precisely the same argument can be used in relation to McAdoo's exposition of the supposed distinction between system and method. It is quite apparent, indeed he openly states it, that the appeal of seventeenth-century theologians to antiquity was designed to show that 'undifferentiated Catholicism was the pivotal point for Anglican thinking' (p.v.) And this obviously includes substantive doctrinal commitment. Whatever the meaning which is attached by McAdoo to the word 'system' when he denies that Anglicanism is a theological system, it certainly cannot mean, if he is to be consistent, that Anglicanism is distinguished by the affirmation of no particular doctrinal content.

The word 'system' is evidently part of the trouble, as we have already seen from Temple's confusing use of the term. What McAdoo believes he is denying in saying that Anglicanism has no system are the following:

(1) that there is no specifically Anglican corpus of doctrine
(2) that Anglicans have no master theologian to compare with Calvin
(3) that there is no tendency to stress specific doctrines (such as predestination)

(4) that there is no tendency to stress one or other of the specific philosophies such as Thomism or nominalism.[4]

To some extent we have already dealt with the very different issues which these points raise, but so prevalent and so influential is this view that it would be as well to reiterate the position which is being defended here.

(1) It is contradictory to say that there is no specifically Anglican corpus of doctrines and also to say that Anglicans regard the teaching of the undivided Church of the first five centuries as a criterion. For something to be 'specifically Anglican' it is quite sufficient that it be *necessary* to the characterisation of Anglicanism. It need not be a *sufficient* characterisation. The confusion here is a common one. All the characteristics specific to a particular thing are what serve to identify it, whether or not the characteristics are common to more than one kind of thing. A fountain-pen has certain specific characteristics, all of which are relevant in distinguishing it from a quill or a ball point pen. It would be ridiculous to say that a quill is not distinct from a fountain-pen because both have nibs, or that a fountain-pen is not distinct from a ball-point because both have containers holding ink. A specific characteristic does not need to be a unique characteristic. What is specific to Anglicanism does not have to be unique to Anglicanism. Not all the characteristics of Anglicanism have to be different from all the characteristics of (say) Orthodoxy for Anglicanism to qualify as a distinct denomination. For an Anglican, therefore, to claim that the Christian faith is sufficiently contained in the reference to the Bible and the faith of the undivided church is a highly characteristic Anglican claim, both in what it says and what it leaves unsaid. There are, therefore, no good grounds for denying that there is a specifically Anglican corpus of doctrine.

(2) The fact that Anglicans have no master theologian is, as I have argued above, irrelevant to the question of whether the specific Anglican position on matters of faith can be developed systematically. Moreover it ignores the fact that generations of protestant theologians have written systematic theologies for their churches with only passing references to Calvin. Schleiermacher, indeed, wrote his *Christian Faith* specifically for a united church, and large numbers of subsequent theologians might be said to defer to him rather than to Calvin or Luther.

(3) The stressing of specific doctrines is hardly a character-

istic of systematic theology. Indeed the interpretation of Calvin is controversial precisely on this point, and reputable scholars believe that Calvin has no 'central doctrine' of this kind.[5] Karl Barth's *Church Dogmatics* is also characterized by the firm denial that there is one doctrine more important than another.

(4) Again the stressing of specific philosophies is characteristic only of the Roman Catholic church's attitude to Thomism, and is not a necessary characteristic of systematic theology *per se*. Indeed the use of the last two points suggest that there is being perpetuated here the same confusion about the term 'system' as characterised Temple's Introduction to the Doctrine Report. 'System' can be applied either to the sum of a specific dogmatic content or to an articulated systematic theology written by a specific individual. My position is that Anglicanism has a specific content, and that it ought to expose that content to examination and criticism; it ought also to encourage specific individuals to write systematic theologies or extended treatments of Christian doctrine (as indeed, Professor John Macquarrie and John Austin Baker have done). These, if they are articulated on a rigorous basis will certainly include the treatment of matters of epistemology and metaphysics, and to this extent they will involve recognisable positions on philosophical matters. There *ought* to be Anglican systematic theologies, that is, theologies of high standards of internal consistency written by Anglicans of conviction. No one will expect such theologies to be awarded the accolade of being *the* Anglican systematics, any more than the work of Karl Rahner or of Karl Barth is spoken of as *the* Catholic systematics or *the* Reformed systematics.

It is evident from the examination of McAdoo's statements, that he wishes to state that Anglicans profess unchanged the faith professed by the primitive church.[6] This position has strong support in a very large number of Anglican statements of considerable authority. But one of the main problems which such a position has to answer is, does this specifically Anglican claim include or exclude the positions of men like Rashdall or, in more modern days, Anglican theologians who do not regard the creeds or the consensus of the fathers as binding. This raises not just a disciplinary question, but a fundamental question about the *method* which it is said is characteristic of Anglicanism. There are those who argue that modern study of the New Testament documents does not permit us to say with

any confidence how Jesus understood his person and mission.
They go on to assert that such uncertainty ought to make us
'less confident in our talk about the special relationship of the
man Jesus to God, which has been the primary form taken by
traditional christological affirmations'.[7] Now it is important
to notice the appeal to historical scholarship here. What is said
to be impossible, is to affirm at one and the same time that our
knowledge of Jesus is historically tentative and uncertain, and
also that this particular historical individual is the embodiment
of the divine. 'Any absoluteness implicit in the concept of an
incarnate divine being is necessarily dissipated by the tentative-
ness of our knowledge of his life and words' (p.49). Is this, or
is this not, and example of the Anglican concern for *history* and
historical scholarship in operation? Whether Professor Wiles is
right or wrong to try to create a sort of christology on the basis
of minimal historical information (talk about 'the transforming
power and significance of the figure of Jesus in human life')[8]
is secondary to the question of method. What happens if
historical study undermines the confidence with which one can
make the affirmations about Christ made by the early church?
The issue has certainly been with us for 100 years. But is there
any evidence that this supposedly distinctive Anglican theological
method has shown any convincing way of handling the question?

Here I wish to refer to some comments of Bishop Richard
Hanson, in a paper specifically on the comprehensiveness of
Anglicanism contributed to discussions with Orthodox theologians. Anglican theological method could be said to be, he
believes, primarily a historical one. 'Its first and main aim is to
study the historical documents relevant to the subject in hand
as thoroughly as possible, and their historical background, and
from there to advance, tentatively and slowly and sometimes
uncertainly, to forming hypotheses or theories or doctrines'.[9]
This method (which one may comment, was also expressly
avowed by William Sanday) can usefully operate as a safeguard
against doctrinaire rigidity and intransigent dogmatism. But
then Hanson goes on to state:

> 'All Anglicans share a similar dogmatic basis, even though it
> might be considered a rather narrow one. All Anglicans are
> united in accepting the dogmatic tradition of the Church up to
> 451. This is as true of the most daring modernist (who will
> want to reinterpret, but not abandon dogma, *vide* Rashdall)
> as it is of the most conservative evangelical.'

He follows this with a series of personal statements about the wisdom of recognising the dogmas of the Trinity and of the incarnation, and affirms his belief that the basis of a future unity of churches will lie in the sharing of the tradition of the church of the first four general councils.

But the proper question to ask is why acceptance of this tradition is not itself a piece of doctrinaire rigidity and intransigent dogmatism. We should ask why, if Anglicans are supposed to operate the historical method outlined earlier, they should not stop, with Maurice Wiles, well short of the kind of confidence which led to the introduction of the *homoousios* (of one substance) clause in the creed. This dogmatic confidence is precisely the thing of which Wiles thinks historical scholarship robs us. Which is true, then, on Hanson's terms? That Wiles is operating a non-Anglican method, or that he is coming to non-Anglican conclusions?

The existence of Wiles' view in the penumbra of scholarly Anglican opinion (and he is very far from being alone in this matter) forces us to ask whether Hanson's understanding of a distinctive Anglican theological method is adequate. For if one, such as Wiles, whose speciality is, precisely, the study of the patristic period, reaches the conclusions we have quoted, it can hardly be said that he did so without giving proper weight to the careful study of the documents of the early church. Notable, moreover, in Hanson's statement is the specific inclusion of Rashdall as one who reinterpreted dogma, but did not abandon it. Others, as we have seen, regard Rashdall with less benevolence. If Rashdall is to be included, one might ask, could not anyone also be included who states, as does Wiles, that he takes the creeds 'very seriously'?[10] Or, if one distinguishes between faith and theology, could one not say that one assents to the faith *in* the creeds, meaning their 'essential content' but in reinterpreted form?

The problem with such a statement is that it begins to be not entirely frank. An Orthodox theologian reading the words, 'All Anglicans are united in accepting the dogmatic tradition of the Church up to 451', might be forgiven for supposing that this included the public confession of the dogmas of the Trinity and Incarnation in a form closely in agreement with that in which Athanasius, or Gregory of Nazianzus or Augustine of Hippo would have spoken of them. At the very least he would be entitled to assume unqualified acceptance of the credal statements, especially of the *homoousios* clause. But in fact what a number of Anglican theologians are saying can be put quite differently. They are saying that the creeds and the theology of the past of the church were the form which the faith took in the cultural context of the past; and this, they neither affirm nor deny. Because of the difficulty of assuming with any kind of integrity that the words of the past can be our words, we ought not to impose them as though they could function in our quite different world as criteria for but necessarily changing beliefs.[11] This position is one which the Report on *Christian Believing* states quite categorically should not be ruled out, as a tenable view within the Church of England. All I wish to point out is that Hanson's representations to the Orthodox church on behalf of Anglicanism seems to me to state something different. And it is unsatisfactory for public documents of this kind to be so at variance with each other.

That, however, is merely to attend to the discrepancy and to provide nothing by way of comment on the substantial point at issue. I wish, therefore, to offer two reflections.

First, I believe that some of the difficulties into which the Anglican church has fallen over these issues of historical scholarship stem directly from its unwillingness to say without equivocation that it has a particular doctrinal position. In fact, of course, successive Lambeth conferences have issued statements which have specific doctrinal content. Sometimes the wording of the statements has been generalised and rhetorical; at other times it has been exceedingly careful. But in principle it is not at all difficult to discover, from a careful perusal of both what has been said and what has been left unsaid, that distinctive positions have been adopted. There is no reason at all why a sophisticated statement of the Anglican position should not distinguish between the public faith of the church, made clear in such pronouncements and incorporated in its liturgy and canon law, and the freedom it extends to scholars, in the name of historical and theological enquiry, to provoke discussion of items of that publicly proclaimed faith. Nor is there any reason why Anglicans should conceal the fact that the doctrinal position has changed. There is no merit in disguising this fact under the cloak of 'reinterpretation'. It ought to be possible to explain and examine the reasons why, under the impact of biblical criticism and theological discussion, the church loosened its official relationship towards the Thirty Nine Articles and the creeds. At the same time it ought to be possible for it to explain why (if this indeed is the case) the doctrine of the Incarnation is the basis of its doctrinal standpoint.

Secondly, I would wish to establish the fact (for so I believe it to be) that all theological method is intrinsically related to particular theological content. The reason for this can be put somewhat summarily as follows: The subject matter of theological method is the explanation of how man can be said to have knowledge of God or to come to understand divine revelation. But what man is is itself part of the content of Christian doctrine. Therefore any understanding of theological method implies a particular theological doctrine or doctrines.

I would be possible, I believe, to show this in a number of examples. Interesting in this connection is the position of Schleiermacher, who despite the fact that he thought that theological method was *not* part of the substance of theology, nonetheless understood the accomplishing of the salvation of man in a way which exactly matches the statements about man's innate religious self-consciousness developed in the methodology. Tillich, who recognises this point precisely, speaks of the correlation of the analysis of existence which informs rationality and the theological answers of the Christian tradition. Barth provides the most obvious example of the relation of method and content, in that the place assigned in most protestant dogmatics to methodology is occupied in his *Church Dogmatics* by an analysis of the relevance of the doctrine of the Trinity for any human claim to be speaking of God.

These are examples drawn from protestant theology; but it would not be difficult to adduce ones also from the history of Roman Catholic thought. It could be argued of Thomas Aquinas himself that, whatever the sources for his understanding of human knowing, that analysis of knowing underlies both his method in the *Summa* and his doctrine of salvation. In modern catholic writing. Karl Rahner has explicitly defined theology as transcendental anthropology, and related the method of theology at every stage to the nature of man so understood. In Lonergan's work the verdict is ambiguous. On the one hand, his *Method in Theology* claims to be merely the application to theology of a transcendental method true of any form of human enquiry whatsoever. On the other hand, it is explicitly stated that all the sorts of specialised work in theology are interdependent, and that natural theology must be understood to be part of systematic theology. At the very least, therefore, the understanding of man which lies at the root of transcendental method is consistent with the man whose highest vocation is the unrestricted love of God. 'Just as unrestricted questioning is our capacity for self-transcendence, so being in love in an unrestricted fashion is the proper fulfilment of that capacity'.[12]

This brief reference to some modern theologians is necessary in order to illustrate the fact that some of the Anglican claims to a distinctive theological method which we have examined are, in their generality, rather remote from the current way in which the question of theological method is discussed by theologians both protestant and Roman Catholic. There is no particular virtue in this remoteness. If it were the case that one could point to several Anglican works explaining and pursuing an independent method, one would be able to discuss the claim more satisfactorily. But one cannot do so because the examples are lacking. One exception we have noted to the general dearth of Anglican systematic theology is Macquarrie's *Principles of Christian Theology*. But here, so it seems to me, the methodology is in substantial agreement with the positions of both Tillich and Rahner, namely that both Macquarrie's understanding of human knowing, in respect of which he expressly reflects themes developed in modern existentialism, and his presentation of the gift of salvation, are directly correlated the one to the other. In this work, at least, no question of a distinctively Anglican method seems to arise.

The conclusion of the chapter can be put as follows: the attempts we have examined at specifying a distinctively Anglican method in theology turn out either to involve considerable commitments as to content, or else to imply the rejection of some of the work of recent Anglican theologians. But in an earlier chapter I argued that the Anglican church has both a distinctive standpoint and a distinctive way of communicating that standpoint. This earlier argument, which appears to require the conclusion that there exists both distinctive content and method in Anglicanism, has now to be brought into relation to what is said here. I propose to do so by pointing out the distinction between the standpoint of the Anglican church (which is evident in its liturgies and canon law) and the writings of its theologians. The Anglican church has a standpoint, whether or not its theologians are aware of it and are prepared to think carefully and critically about it. But if and when they do so, they will write what can and should be called 'Anglican theology', which will be recognisably Anglican both as to content and to method. In other words if there is Anglican theology there will be Anglican method — but in both cases it will be the work of individual theologians, writing in the service of their communion and not as though legislating for it.

This conclusion ought to cause no surprise, since it is identical with the understanding of the relation of a systematic theologian to his communion as that developed by the distinguished Roman Catholic, Bernard Lonergan, in his *Method in Theology*. Lonergan helpfully enables one to see both that there is a general methodology applicable to any intellectual endeavour whatsoever, and also that there are specific procedures which must be followed as soon as certain fundamental decisions have been taken about the conflicts which arise in theology. He writes as an individual Roman Catholic systematic theologian, related in the closest way to the specific content of the Roman Catholic standpoint, and thus also to the theological methods correlated with that content. If my argument is correct about the existence of a discernible Anglican standpoint emerging from its liturgy and canon law, then it follows that there should exist a genre of Anglican theological literature corresponding to Roman Catholic systematic theology. If such literature does not exist, then I can only imagine three explanations; it may be that Anglicans have special insight into why the whole enterprise of systematic theology is a waste of time — in which case one ought to be able to point to some substantial controversial writing in which the labours of Tillich, Barth, Pannenberg, Moltmann, Jüngel, Rahner, Lonergan and other modern systematicians, are shown to be deficient in conception. But so far from this being the case, we would more easily be able to show how pathetically grateful Anglicans are to have some writing on which to cut their theological teeth and how parasitic Anglican theological education is on the existence of such literature. Or secondly, it may be that my argument about the existence of an Anglican standpoint is fallacious. And in this case I hope it will not be long before its errors have been exposed. Or, thirdly, and I can see no further possibilities, it may be that the contemporary Anglican communion is in gross dereliction of its duty to foster the critical study of its own standpoint as a church participating in the universal Church of Christ, to its own impoverishment and to the impoverishment of its contribution to the cause of Christian unity.

FOOTNOTES

1. *Theology* Vol XLVIII (1945), p.2
2. *The Spirit of Anglicanism* (London, 1965)
3. *From Gore to Temple* p. 90
4. *The Spirit of Anglicanism*, p. 1, and *Being an Anglican* (Dublin and London, 1977)
5. François Wendel, *Calvin* (London, 1965; Fontana edn.) pp. 357f
6. *Being an Anglican*, p. 10
7. M. F. Wiles, *The Remaking of Christian Doctrine* (London, 1974) p. 50
8. *Christian Believing*, p. 129
9. R. P. C. Hanson, 'A Marginal Note on Comprehensiveness, *Theology*, Vol LXXV, p. 631
10. *Christian Believing*, p. 125
11. *Christian Believing*, pp. 36f
12 B. J. F. Lonergan, *Method in Theology* (London, 1972) p. 106

Chapter 6

ANGLICANS AND THE THEOLOGY OF THE CHURCH

A CAREFUL inspection of the literature reveals that it could not be said without qualification that Anglicans have failed to attend to the doctrine of the church. That would be to overlook the contribution of a number of writers in this century, among them, Gore, Quick, Lionel Thornton, Mascall, Dillistone, Pittinger and Neill. The books are undeniably there on the shelves, even if they are not much read. The failure of contemporary Anglicanism is rather the failure to foster this study in such a way, for example, that the implications for ecclesiology of a report like *Christian Believing* would have been immediately obvious, both to the members of the commission itself and to Anglican church leaders generally. It may be that this is, strictly speaking, a failure of the late 1960s and 1970s, which the present generation of younger Anglican theologians ought to consider with great seriousness. But even if the situation is of comparatively recent date, I believe that the basic causes lie deep in the history of Anglican theological scholarship.

A number of reasons can be advanced for any deficiencies in respect of the doctrine of the church, and indeed for systematic theology generally:

(1) Anglicans have not attached great importance to systematic theology, but have justified the position of the Anglican church more on practical than on theoretical grounds. Those who wish to find explanations and justification of Anglicanism will find them in the letters and papers of the great modern Anglican leaders rather than in heavy tomes of scholarship.[1]

(2) The circumstances of the establishment of theological faculties in the universities of England have led to the neglect of systematic theology especially ecclesiology, compared with the development of historical and philosophical theology; and the situation in Anglican theological colleges has been such as effectively to inhibit scholarship.

(3) The consequence of the tension between Anglo-Catholics and Evangelicals in the nineteenth century was to make ecclesiology a highly controversial topic; and the theory of

'agreement on fundamentals', traditionally held by Anglicans, meant, when applied to this conflict that ecclesiology must belong to the non-fundamentals. This partly unconscious process of relegation was accompanied by a vigorous affirmation of the institution of the threefold ministry, based, however, on very controversial historical argument.

Each of those reasons must now be examined in greater detail. (1) The first reason, the general Anglican disinclination to attach great importance to systematic theology, has been briefly touched on in the last section, but obviously deserves closer scrutiny. Frequently cited in this respect is the lack of a dominant theologian in the history of the Anglican reformation, a lack which modern writers gloss as an advantage in as much as Anglicanism has never been 'cramped theologically within the narrow mould of the specific theology of any one particular teacher'.[2] It is, of course, a liberation that Anglicans have been saved the necessity of tediously showing how each new movement derives from some element of the major teacher's vision. Seminal mind though he may have been, Luther has been credited with being the inspiration of an improbably large number of modern theological tendencies. Similarly, Anglicans may be forgiven the liberty of doubting whether the totality of theological wisdom has been bestowed in the combined writings of the Greek fathers. To this extent it is perfectly true that to be identifiably Anglican in one's theology one does not need to lace one's writings with references to one or other of the Anglican reformers. But there is a negative side to this. Uncramped though they may have been, Anglicans have also lacked the theological stimulus of having to wrestle with the theological writing of a great Christian teacher. In earlier days, it would have been possible to assert that the fathers of the Greek and Latin churches up to the Council of Chalcedon played this role, and that Anglican theology was greatly stimulated by the practice of patristic study. Indeed there is a very good case for saying that in the late nineteenth century, Anglican theology was at its most stimulating in its discussion of the major issues of ecclesiology arising out of patristic study, specifically in relation to the development of ecclesiastical organisation and the threefold ministry, the question of the development of dogma, and the alleged contrast between the Greek and the Augustinian attitudes towards theology. But it would be a bold man who would claim any such position for patristic study in modern Anglicanism. Nor is it possible to identify any more recent writers, with the possible (and dubious) exception of F. D. Maurice, to whom large numbers of Anglicans seem to look as a guide into the profundities of theological thought. Liberating though this may be in one way, we must beg leave to suppose that the lack of a history of major theological achievement has not a little to do with the failure of modern Anglicanism to foster any acute awareness of its own theological stance.

That is not all that should be said about the contemporary aversion to systematic theology, and the preference for the practical over the merely theoretical. Another aspect of it is put by Bishop Wand in his influential review of Anglicanism. He writes:

> It is observable that when the strong medicine of continental theology is introduced to Anglican circles it generally suffers considerable dilution before it is accepted for the cure of souls. Anglican theology is too closely allied to the altar and the pulpit to permit of its themes being handled as if they were primarily intended for the lecturer's desk. This has given to Anglican theology a magisterial and judicial quality which may not be as exciting as the qualities demanded of the pioneer and explorer but is probably even more valuable for helping souls in the way of pastoral care.[3]

The problem of relating academic theology to altar and pulpit is not a unique one for Anglicans, however. And the statement that Anglican theologians in particular are obliged to 'dilute' Calvin, Luther, Barth or Bultmann in order to make them valuable for helping souls is simply English parochialism. Major writers of the stature of the aforementioned obviously require (and have acquired) interpreters before their messages can be proclaimed with sufficient simplicity and directness from the chancel steps. These interpreters are as much needed in Germany and Switzerland as they are in England. The question remains, why are there no Anglicans in the list of major theological figures? Given that all major efforts of intellectual endeavour need interpretation before they can be preached (a fact as true of Roman Catholic writers like von Balthasar, Rahner or Lonergan, as it is of the protestants named above), why are there no Anglicans to match the quality of the writing referred to? Can it be that it is actually thought that there is merit in not being theologically sophisticated? The signs of such a view are not far below the surface, oddly though they clash with the much acclaimed Anglican trilogy of scripture, tradition and *reason*. E. C. Hoskyns acutely observed the weakness in the 'characteristic English substitution of piety for theology' in a letter contributed to the *Festschrift* published in honour of Karl Barth's fiftieth birthday.[4] The choice for Anglicans is evidently not between being either theologically profound or pastorally oriented; consideration of the works of Luther or of Rahner and von Balthasar dispose of that fallacy. It is rather between being theologically profound and theologically superficial. The commendation of Anglican theology as 'magisterial and judicial' [sic] has a sadly hollow ring.

(2) The second reason given for general weakness in the performance of Anglicans when it comes to systematic theology is domestic to the Church of England, and lies in the circumstances attending the establishment of theological faculties in British universities. In the mid-nineteenth century, when the theological faculties of both Oxford and Cambridge were set up, it seems that it was thought right that there should be a heavy predominance of scriptural study. The reason for this fact lies in part, in the terms of Article VI of the Thirty-Nine Articles, which states, 'Holy Scripture containeth all things necessary to salvation'. At the time, however, because of the acute controversy over the question of the extent to which any examination in theology was bound to take cognisance of the orthodoxy, as well as the learning, of the answers, the tendency was (and with each liberalisation of the university was reinforced) to lay heavy emphasis on the *historical* interpretation of these and other admittedly authoritative texts. Hence, although in Oxford in 1870 there was a paper entitled *'Dogmatic and Symbolic Theology'*, in 1904 the content of the paper became identical with the history of Christian Doctrine to 451 AD.[5] In effect the curriculum of both Oxford and Cambridge Theological Faculties has been for 70 years non-denominational, but with an implicit bias towards the literary and historical interpretation of texts (scriptural and patristic) regarded as uniquely authoritative by Anglicans. To this programme of study one must add the discipline of 'Evidences', now spoken of as philosophical theology or philosphy of religion, whose subject matter is the epistemology of Christian theology and certain problems of

general philosophical interest, arising out of Christian theism (the existence of God, evil, prayer, miracles and providence). But for 70 years, at least, no systematic or dogmatic theology has been taught. It seems, then, that in so far as Anglican theology has been nurtured in Oxford and Cambridge (and that is to a considerable extent) it has been nurtured by a curriculum innocent of a direct cultivation of important theological disciplines.

Stray remarks in the writings of theologians and churchmen of the period are revealing. When in 1933 C. C. J. Webb published a book on *Religious Thought in England from 1850*, he made it clear at the first opportunity that by 'Religious Thought' he meant philosophy of religion. In a passage on his quest for a sound intellectual basis for belief, Dean Inge recalled how, having despaired of an infallible scripture and an infallible church, he turned to mysticism and philosophy.[6] This generation knew little of the methods of modern systematic theology, and, on the few occasions on which they can be found to refer to them, they not infrequently make simplistic remarks about 'subjectivism' or 'dogmatism'.

There is, however, no good reason for Anglicans to hold aloof from systematic theology. The historical accident of the neglect of systematics in the universities of Oxford and Cambridge does much to account for the poverty of Anglican scholarship in this direction. We do not need to gloss this fact with the oft-repeated excuse that 'English people do not love system or order or completeness'.[7] If that were true, the outstanding achievements of English scientists would be unintelligible. The fact is that academic establishments have an insidious way of trying to protect themselves from outside influences. When we consider the similar excuses offered by English philosophers for their ignorance of the writings of Hegel or the existentialists (excuses such as 'the English mind does not think like this', or 'Englishmen are empiricists'), it is evident that what we have here is an educationally reinforced preference for analytic thought, and a prejudice against metaphysics, of comparatively recent origin. Change the educational environment and, miraculously, one discovers that the English can make as much sense as Hegel or of Marx or of Kierkegaard or of Sartre as anyone else, and, moreover, that an Englishman can be taught to appreciate the points for which each one was striving.

It emerges, too, that some outstanding thinkers have been able to transcend the boundaries artificially erected on national lines, for example, that the Austrian Wittgenstein was stimulated by both Russell and Kierkegaard. The excuses for intellectual parochialism look not merely thin, but are evidence of a basically second-rate quality, like the feeble reasons which were initially raised against the study of Kant.[8]

But the neglect of systematic theology in the universities also partly accounts for its neglect in the seminary training of Anglican ordinands. For the teachers themselves, never having been taught the discipline, found neither the impetus nor the time to devote themselves to the proper cultivation of systematics outside the university. Instead Anglican ordinands were educated in Anglican theology by means of commentaries on the Thirty Nine Articles or dogmatic handbooks, of a more or less ecclesiastically partisan character. I do not wish to give the impression that this was wasted time. Certainly some of the commentators were substantial theologians, learned in the history of the Anglican church, and offering reasoned cases for their theological stances. Any Anglican ordinand who had mastered one such of these books would not come naked to a discussion, say, of the status of ecumenical councils in the Church of England, as, one fears, a modern Anglican student would do. But precisely because as commentaries they were bound to follow the text these works had severe methodological limits. And it is also to be feared that neither they, nor the handbooks of dogma also available, were capable of training men to see what might be involved in thinking through the subject matter of Christian theology in a consistent way.

And it must be added that the theological colleges themselves, dominated as many of them were and still are by specific ecclesiastical commitments, were prone to appoint safe party men in preference to scholars. The total output of scholarship from the staff of these colleges, especially in dogmatic or systematic theology, is scandalously meagre, the scandal being the fact that in this area the universities were comparatively inactive (as compared with their commitments to biblical studies, patristics, or ecclesiastical history). But no recognition seems to be given to the fact that a member of staff cannot produce works of high systematic quality on the basis of no prior training, unless he is endowed with adequate resources, especially of time. Too often promising young men have been appointed, and then loaded with teaching duties covering an impossibly wide spectrum. The result is as we see it today. Not merely is there no tradition of systematic theology in the Church of England, there is no recognition of the part it could play in fostering a critical self-understanding without which no church is truly alive.

One final point may be made, which is the confusion still prevalent even in informed minds between the history of doctrine and systematic theology. For a long time it could be assumed that the study of patristics would raise all the major issues of systematic theology, and (it might be thought) solve them. Eventually, however, it was discovered that patristics could be treated (as any part of intellectual history) in a more or less purely historical manner. Reformation theology and history likewise tended to be annexed to the discipline of ecclesiastical history. Hence, if the traditional link between the study of historical theology and some kind of constructive theology was to preserved it would have to be by reference to the history of modern theology. Thus it came about that in some quarters the term 'modern theology' came to do duty for systematics, and the tacit assumption made that systematics was covered if 'modern theology' appeared on the curriculum. This, however, is a superstition. It is, of course, very difficult to do systematic theology where a student has little or no knowledge of the history of Christian doctrine. But the historical study of doctrine is a subject in its own right, requiring a wide knowledge of general intellectual history, especially the history of philosophy and of the church as a social institution. Courses on 'Christian Doctrine', which have largely figured in the curricula both of universities and theological colleges, have led, it is to be feared, to a confusion of thought on this issue. Students have, in effect, been invited to do the impossible, namely to master the outlines of the history of theology, and to work on the problems and methods of systematic theology, at one and the same time. At worst doctrine has been covertly turned into the history of doctrine, as a kind of escape from the intellectual demands of a consistent approach to constructive theology. At best little justice has been done to either. This, too, is a thoroughly unsatisfactory situation, and an indirect inheritance of a set of circumstances which have dominated and distorted the educational arrangements of the Church of England for too long, to its evident impoverishment.

(3) The last of the reasons for the lack of Anglican theology accounts, in part, for the specific contemporary failure in respect of ecclesiology. The nineteenth century saw a great increase in overt tension between the anglo-catholic and the evangelical wings in the Church of England, and this led to a considerable literature, often of a polemical character on the main points of controversy vis-a-vis the church, ministry and sacraments, such topics as episcopal ordination, baptismal regeneration, and the presence of Christ in the eucharistic elements. As has already been mentioned, Anglicans cultivated, too, a considerable literature on the ecclesiology of the fathers, some of which was of an internally polemical character or written to controvert Roman Catholic apologists in the tradition of Newman.

Parallel with this, and ultimately at odds with the attention accorded these questions, was the long-standing tradition of Anglican apologetic which insisted that all Anglicans held the fundamentals of the faith in common. Manifestly if this were true, then the implication of profound conflict over the church between anglo-catholic and evangelical was that ecclesiology was not a fundamental doctrine. Acceptable though this might be to an evangelical, and especially to a broad churchman, it was manifestly unacceptable to anglo-catholics. We see this clearly in the attempt by a group of prominent Anglicans of anglo-catholic sympathies to substitute for the idea of agreement on 'fundamentals', stigmatised as 'superficial platitudes about our common Christianity', the quite different notion of 'the recovery of wholeness'.[9] The study of the report of this group is most enlightening in this connection, since its findings entailed an explicit identification of the 'radical errors' of protestantism, the fatal 'man-centredness' of liberal Christianity and 'faults' of post-Tridentine Roman Catholicism. Criticising 'certain commonly held ideas of 'comprehensiveness', this report urges Anglicans to seek for a synthesis which 'involves not a mere inclusion of diverse opinions but an embracing of the positive truths of our tradition in their depth and vigour' (pp. 51 f). This overt support given to Maurice's reformulation of the theory of the *Via Media* is perfectly understandable in the light of the principal aim of the report. This was to establish the anglo-catholic view of the church as one of the 'positive truths' which could on no account be lost in any future synthesis. The anglo-catholic doctrine of the church, with its exalted view of episcopacy, could certainly not be said to have been part of the fundamentals of the faith, as understood by generations of Anglicans since the reformation. It could scarcely even be said to have been guarded by the Lambeth Quadrilateral of 1888, with its bare reference to the historic episcopate. The report, therefore, does not hesitate to gloss the terms of the Quadrilateral, in accord with its own theory of wholeness. It states:

> 'The appeal to the *historic Episcopate* will mean the recovery of the true place of the Bishop in the Church, not as the organiser of a vast administrative machine, but as the guardian and exponent of the faith, as the bond of sacramental unity, and as an organ of the Body of Christ in true constitutional relation to the presbyters and people' (pp. 54 f.)

This statement, together with the parting shot that there are some Anglicans who regard parts of the one single pattern of Anglicanism to be of its *esse* which others do not regard as of its *esse*, is a direct challenge to the traditional theory of fundamentals, and an attempt to rewrite the terms of Anglican comprehensiveness to make it synonymous with the report's own theory of wholeness or catholicity.

How is this to be evaluated? The obvious difficulty it at once creates is the account given of the ecclesial life of Christians in non-episcopal churches. Furthermore there is a historical difficulty in connecting the apostles with the leadership of the primitive church. Are there good historical grounds for supposing that there were expected to be 'successors to the apostles'? Some biblical and historical defences of this suggestion have been very severely handled. There is also a problem of method which we should note. While it is true that Anglicans have consistently defended the retention of episcopacy for a variety of reasons, it is an innovation to suggest that Anglicans have regarded any particular theological interpretation of episcopacy as essential. This, indeed, is why Maurice's understanding of the complementarity of aspects of the truth is invoked by the authors of *Catholicity* This theory, we should notice, enables *any* group of Anglicans to claim that their particular understanding of a theological doctrine should never be compromised. But if that theory is invalid, then the stance on episcopacy which the report adopts, with its notable lack of reference to those doctrines which historically Anglicans have regarded as included in the fundamentals, is markedly weakened.

In the end the most one can say is that this is a matter about which some Anglicans feel strongly. And of all such matters the correct question to ask is, with what cogency can the case be made for their view? The trouble is that, popularly, the issue has become divorced from historical and theological scholarship, and the consequence of this has been a perhaps unconscious devaluation of the status of ecclesiology. But the discussion does not deserve to be polarized in this way. The historic Anglican position is acceptance of the institution of episcopacy and of the two Gospel sacraments, but toleration of disagreement on their interpretation; and it needs to be said this toleration is itself a highly significant ecclesiological matter. It is not to be dismissed with contempt as woolly compromise of no theological significance. If the argument of the proceeding sections is valid, that which is carefully left unspecified is left unspecified for reasons which may be bad or good, but which, in either case, ought to be examined. Ultimately, on this view, it is unacceptable to say that these factors, like the desire to avoid controversy, are 'non-theological'. So long as they are consciously related to the life of the Christian Church they should be classed as theological; which is not to say that the theology implied is correct. The advantage of recognising them as theological considerations is that they may be subjected to theological argument, criticism and appraisal.

In summary: The weakness of modern Anglican ecclesiology may be in part traced to the disrepute into which certain passionately held dogmas fell when exposed to historical criticism; but it must also be traced to the chronic reluctance of Anglicans to accept the fact that what they have inherited as institutions and practices in the church unencumbered with sharply defined theoretical baggage has profound theological, especially ecclesiological significance *as such*. And it is only the theological exploration of the significance of such an inheritance which will begin to establish Anglicanism on lines significant for the future of the world-wide church, not on the bogus grounds of its status as a so-called 'bridge church', but on the grounds of its capacity to submit its inheritance to a searching theological appraisal.

FOOTNOTES

1. cf. J.W.C. Wand, *Anglicanism in History and Today* (London, 1961) p. 253, where this view is expressed.

2. A.E.J. Rawlinson, *The Genius of the Church of England* (London, 1947) p. 10.

3. *Anglicanism in History and Today*, p. 228.

4. *Theologische Aufsätze* (, 1935) p. 528.

5. See David Jenkins, 'Oxford—The Anglican Tradition', in J. Coulson (ed) *Theology and the University* (London, 1964) pp. 146-162.

6. W.R. Inge, *Vale* (London, 1934) pp. 32f.

7. A.C. Headlam's apology for the lack of Anglican works of theology, at the opening of his own work of systematic theology, *Christian Theology* (Oxford, 1934), p. 4.

8. For example, by Henry Crabb Robinson, *Diary Reminiscences and Correspondence*, Vol III (London, 1869) p. 91.

9. *Catholicity* (London, 1947). The Liberal Evangelical reply interestingly and significantly returns to the theory of essential doctrines, *The Fulness of Christ* (London, 1950).

Chapter 7

AUTHORITY IN ANGLICANISM

I THINK it will not unreasonably be said of what has been written hitherto that it is mainly critical and destructive, reflecting my deep sense of the inherent contradiction in Anglicanism as it has developed over the last few years, and the inadequacy of conventional Anglican apologetic to do justice to the real situation. I wish now, however, to tackle what seems to me the central issue, the question of authority in the Church of England, in a way which will, I hope, illustrate the kind of presuppositions lying behind the criticisms contained in the earlier sections. The usual Anglican writing on this topic approaches the question from the point of view of the norms of authority, scripture, tradition and reason, not infrequently with a complacent sidelong glance at Ecclesiastes 4:12; 'a threefold cord is not quickly broken'. The problem with this approach is its ambiguity, especially in respect of the third member of the trio. What, after all, is rationality in theology? The answers to this are as various as Christendom itself. The arrogation of great learning (or, more implausibly still, great wisdom) to the contemporary Anglican church is, if only few of the criticisms developed earlier are true, spectacularly inappropriate. Rationality, of course, would be claimed by the authoritative structures of any Christian church, and it is only when it is specified with the aid of other particular attitudes that anything like an Anglican position begins to emerge.

By far the most considerable statement on authority in Anglicanism to be found in official Anglican documentation is contained in a section of the 1948 Lambeth Conference Report (printed in the Appendix). This states that authority is both singular, in that it derives from the mystery of the divine Trinity, and plural, in that it is distributed in numerous, organically related elements. Employing an analogy with scientific method, which is a theme expanded by Lonergan in his *Method in Theology*, the document sees the elements in authority as an ongoing process of describing the data, ordering them, mediating and verifying them. This 'dispersed authority' is a mutually supporting, and mutually checking, life-process, in which the temptations to tyranny and the dangers of unhampered power can be resisted. In respect of Anglicanism, the report claims (with perhaps, at this point, too little explanation), this authority is reflected in adherence to episcopacy as 'the source and centre of our order' and the Book of Common Prayer. But it is significantly stated that the crucible in which these elements of authority are fused in liturgy, the offering and ordering of the public worship of God in the power of the Holy Spirit and in the presence of the living and ascended Christ.

This I believe to be the most satisfactory public statement of the Anglican view of authority, and while it, too, has to be expanded and elucidated in certain respects, it remains, of lasting value. Especially significant, in my opinion, is the implicit recognition of the probability of conflict. In the plurality of the elements of authority, the Report states, Anglicans recognise 'God's loving provision against the temptations to tyranny and the dangers of unchecked power'. It is, I believe, one of the chief weaknesses of the documents of the Second Vatican Council that it conspicuously fails to expect conflict in the church. Whereas there is much evidence of conscious response to the heightened sense of personal maturity and responsibility which is the chief product of the growth of education in democratic society, there is an incomplete, even an unrealistic, expectation of what such a new situation will entail. The manifold conflicts which have fallen on the post-Vatican II Roman Catholic church seem, initially at least, to have caused the leadership surprise and distress. The very processes of consultation which the Council recommended are themselves the agencies which generate conflict. And while the documents elevate the episcopate in a remarkable way, to counterbalance, it may be, the authority of the Pope, they also initiate developments which ensure that every educated Roman Catholic will learn how and why episcopal decisions are made, and consider himself to be competent to follow (and, obviously, to assess) the reasoning behind them. Because of the tradition of Roman Catholic ecclesiology, however, there is no explicit or systematic development of any such 'dispersal' of authority as is formulated by the 1948 Lambeth Report. Nonetheless, if I have read the situation aright, in practice, by the recognition of the significance of personal responsibility, the Council has liberated the Roman church from a long tradition of reactionary rejection of the

European enlightenment and initiated a development which can only lead in due course to a similar dispersal of the elements of authority.

In such a situation the long Anglican history of the experience of conflict is, I believe, of potentially great service. More than one Anglican writer has pointed out that despite the very acute internal disagreements since the nineteenth century there have been extraordinarily few schisms. This feature has also its negative side; a body with very marked internal tensions finds it very difficult to unite with another body, when the very proposals for union will inevitably disturb a carefully (if instinctively) preserved internal balance. For this reason Anglicans ought not to be particularly sanguine about the ecumenical potential in the apparent process of liberalisation in the Roman Catholic church, which will make the problem of reunion more difficult while appearing to be easier. As the Church of England found in its abortive negotiations with Methodists, an internally disunited body cannot achieve reunion by committee. Decision-making becomes a cumbersome business and subject to the activities of unofficial pressure groups wielding specified and unspecified threats. And ultimately the bestowal of voting powers upon large groups of church people creates a heavy balance in favour of the *status quo*. One cannot imagine, for example, the Roman church as a whole voting strongly in favour of the vernacularisation of the liturgy.

A dispersed authority implies recognition of the probability of conflict. This is the starting-point of the position which I wish to develop. Conflict is the presupposed condition of the church of the New Testament, a fact which, in the concentration of modern interest upon the frequently voiced appeals for unanimity, is sometimes overlooked. Conflict can, of course, be virtually eliminated in any human society by the wielding of sufficient power; and the apparatus of threat and coercion has by no means been left idle in the Christian church. It is perfectly true that excommunication was envisaged in the New Testament church, and that, particularly in the later documents (for example, 2 and 3 John and 2 Peter), it is associated not merely with moral offences but with unorthodoxy. Moreover it is perfectly conceivable that under certain conditions, such as when a totalitarian régime requires that the church abandon or distort essential features of the gospel, it might be necessary to distinguish between a true and a false church, in order to preserve the integrity of the faith. But the sort of diversity of which the New Testament gives abundant evidence, and much of the conflict which lies in the background especially of the letters of Paul, requires nothing like the mechanisms to ensure total obedience which the church eventually devised for itself.

It is to this situation that Article VI (of the Thirty Nine Articles), on the sufficiency of the Holy Scriptures for salvation, speaks with such pertinent wisdom.

> 'Holy Scripture containeth all things necessary for salvation: so that whatsoever is not read therein, nor may be proved thereby, is not to be required of any man, that it should be believed as an article of faith, or be thought requisite or necessary to salvation.'

The idea of 'proving' doctrine by scripture has, since the sixteenth century, become much more complex. But the essential point of the Article is clearly the negation on which it insists. It is not saying that everything which can be read in scripture ought to be believed; but rather that what a plain reader cannot himself find in the text can in no circumstances be required of him as an article of belief. This negative is reinforced in Articles XX and XXI on the authority of the church and of general councils, where again it is specifically stated that the church has no authority 'to ordain any thing that is contrary to God's Word written, neither may it so expound one place of scripture, that it be repugnant to another'. These emphatic statements are contextualized by two Anglican reformed practices; that of making copies of the scripture in the vernacular available in the laity, and of reading scripture publicly in the context of worship. This is enshrined in the opening words of Cranmer's preface 'Concerning the Service of the Church', which is itself a revision of a preface to a breviary commissioned by Pope Paul III, but eventually abandoned for its radicalism.

> 'The first original and ground [for Divine Service, writes Cranmer] if a man would search out by the ancient Fathers he shall find, that the same was not ordained but of good purpose, and for a great advancement of godliness.'

(The reference to the fathers is explicitly derived from the revised breviary, and reflects the practice of using bible readings at vigil services in the early church and developed in the monastic movement).

> 'For they so ordained the matter, that all the whole Bible, (or the greatest part thereof) should be read over once every year; intending thereby, that the Clergy, and especially such as were Ministers in the congregation, should (by often reading, and meditation in God's word) be stirred up to godliness themselves, and be more able to exhort others by wholesome doctrine, and to confute them that were adversaries to the truth. And further, [here Cranmer makes his own addition to the text] that the people (by daily hearing of holy Scripture read in the Church) might continually profit more and more in the knowledge of God, and be the more inflamed with the love of his true religion.'

It may be doubted whether the reference to 'daily hearing' was anything more than a pious wish. Cranmer's lectionary has had to be revised, and the framers of new lectionaries have had a considerable problem in ensuring both that there is a sensible arrangement for those who say the services daily, and that the mass of church people hear a satisfactory amount of scripture read on Sundays. The position of scripture reading has been confirmed in modern times. For example, the use of the scriptures in worship was described by the 1958 Lambeth Conference as one of the features most effective in maintaining the traditional doctrinal emphases of the Anglican communion.[1]

The possession by ordinary clergy and by the laity of the means of judgement in matters relating to the integrity of the faith and to the proper preaching of the gospel is crucial for the Anglican understanding of authority. It means that whatever machinery a church may devise for making decisions, and with whatever spiritual powers this machinery may adorn itself, at the end of the day the people of God have the means of judging, independently if need be, whether or not the truth is being upheld. That the scriptures are read in the context of worship is mutually illuminating. Not merely is it the case that the scriptures are interpreted by the performance of the liturgy, but it is also true that the liturgy is interpreted by what the worshipper hears read from scripture. If what is instructed by canon law as an essential element in the liturgy is actually contrary to the clear meaning of scripture, then either this contradiction will eventually become apparent to the worshipper, or else he will subconsciously discount one or other element in it.

To put the matter as I have done is probably to make it seem altogether too simple a process to be entirely credible. An example will reveal the difficulty of making judgements in this area sharp and precise. If we consider the marriage service in the Church of England, it is evident that the revision of 1928, with its rewritten preface and the making optional of the woman's promise of obedience, embodies a substantially different conception of marriage from that maintained in the Book of Common Prayer. When, however, the worshipper hears in the services of the Church the passages relating to marriage from the gospels and epistles, he may very well be led to think that it is the old, rather than the new, form which reflects the meaning of scriptures. Does my contention that ordinary clergy and the laity have the means of judging matters relating to the integrity of the faith by reason of the public reading of the scriptures imply that in due course there ought to be a popular movement to return to the form of service found in the Book of Common Prayer? There are a number of elements in the answer to this question. First, one observes that a number of couples continue to make use of the provision which enables the woman to promise to obey her husband, thus demonstrating the continued appeal of the older tradition, no doubt for a variety of reasons. Secondly, the theological argument against the view of matrimony implied in 'such persons as have not the gift of continency' (words from the introduction to the BCP Marriage Service) is certainly developed in conjunction with an appeal to themes in scripture, especially to the doctrine of creation and to the Old Testament. In other words, we have here not a simple case of scripture versus modern sentiment, but of scripture versus scripture, including the scriptural grounds for allowing Christian doctrine to be responsive to changes in human self-understanding. Thirdly, I think it would be very foolhardy to suggest that we are at present in the position of having resolved the question about the Christian doctrine of marriage. We are, in fact, in the very position which best illustrates what is meant by the Anglican dispersal of authority. The permissive alterations which have been introduced into the Church of England's service books embody, in effect, a process whereby certain theological proposals stemming from the church's leadership have been submitted to a checking process at the hands of the laity. Although the matter has now been in gestation for fifty years and more it is evident that it is far from resolved. Indeed the more intense discussion of the problem of divorce has made the question increasingly complex.

The point which I am concerned to sustain is that it is of the essence of the Anglican view of authority that it should be maintained in principle that the means of judging matters concerning the faith are in the hands of the whole people of God by reason of their access to the Scriptures; and, further, that it is distinctively Anglican that this means is given to them in the liturgy of the church, backed by canon law. I have mounted this argument by reference to some Anglican documents of the sixteenth century. A more fundamental view of the matter is obtained by considering the problem for the early church. Here, too, there are good reasons for the supposing that conflicts would necessarily arise, and call for mature Christian discernment:

(1) Those who preach the gospel are committed to making their meaning plain in words, and words are inherently and necessarily ambiguous. Of any analytic impulse the scriptures are clearly innocent; but the signs of difficulty about the meaning of some of the basic words in Christian vocabulary (consider, for example, 'freedom') are already present. And in due course, with the development of inquiry into the significance of the gospel, the ambiguity inherent in words plays an increasingly important role.

(2) The actions of Jesus were done at a particular time and in particular places, and so are literally unrepeatable. Those who 'follow Christ', therefore, and try to live their own different lives in imitation of him, are necessarily never able to be sure that their actions are 'like' his. All similarity falls short of identity.

(3) The literary deposit about Jesus is, in any case, contained in distinct sources with their own characteristics, and these can be, and were, developed differently in different places.

(4) Although it was believed that Jesus was in the basic sense a complete revelation of God, within that context it was quickly obvious that there were independent sources of knowledge which had existed before Jesus and of which account had to be taken subsequently. Moreover there were questions which had been asked, and answered, for example in medical science,

on which Christians had no specific opinion. The relating of
these different sources of knowlege to the revelation of God in
Christ provided opportunities for diverse theories, and in consequence for controversy.

(5) Especially was this true in relation to 'the problem of
philosophy', which is in reality a nest of different problems.
The early church soon discovered that it had to give some
account of the learning and the art of the ancient world, as
sources of light upon the human situation. The problem of
Christ and culture likewise gave rise to a diversity of solutions.

The inevitability of conflict about the Christian gospel is,
therefore, not a matter of peripheral questions relating to
matters with which only a small number of intellectuals might
be expected to concern themselves. Conflict is present at the
very heart of decisions about the terms of Christian preaching
and the style of Christian living. That the Christian church
changed in the course of the first five centuries and subsequently, cannot be doubted by any serious student of the evidence.
Moreover, hardly anyone now would dispute Newman's contention that if it had not changed, it could not have remained the
same. The question is, did it remain the same? Or did it, in the
course of changing, become subject to distortion either
blatantly, by substitution, or, more covertly, by accretion? In
any case the changes were accompanied by controversy; and
this very controversy reveals what is in fact an unavoidable
problem for the church, namely, that it is possible for wrong
decisions to be made and that one must therefore take the
greatest care. The conclusion must be that authentic Christian
preaching and living can only be achieved in the midst of
ambiguity and with attendant controversy, in which it is the
Christian's duty to exercise careful discernment, if he is not to
go (or be led) astray.

The question which this situation makes urgent is whether
it is right or even conceivable that controversy should be
resolved without reference to the whole of the Christian
community. When the accredited teachers of the church
differed among themselves on a matter of doctrine, as did the
bishops before, during and after the Council of Nicaea in 325
AD, the only way of assuring a speedy resolution was the
employment of the bluntest of weapons, namely political coercion. To establish orthodoxy by imperial legislation, and to

deprive dissidents of their churches, has a certain logical economy about it, in that it ensures that alternative views are never put to the laity. But in practice even these drastic procedures were accompanied by a form of theological argument which was, in principle, accessible to every layman. This argument consisted in an appeal to tradition, that is, to trust in the official preaching and worship of the church as far back as memory or reliable documentation reached. The appeal to tradition is, on analysis, extraordinarily sophisticated, and there is no doubt that it saved the church from the grosser forms of syncretism which threatened it in the very early years. Furthermore it had this characteristic, too, that it ensured that if there was to be deviation from the faith once delivered to the saints it would happen by surreptitious accretion, rather than by the mere fiat of church leaders. In other words, the appeal to tradition contains within itself an element of reference to the memory of the whole Christian community. Jan Coggan, in Hardy's *Far from the Madding Crowd*, who declared he hated 'a feller who'll change his old ancient doctrines for the sake of getting to heaven', is the voice of tradition personified, admonishing the rival theologians of the church from a chair of considerable authority in the kitchen of the Buck's Head.

We can add to this argument the fact that the Christian community as a whole gathers most of what it learns of doctrine from the worship of the church. Liturgies, sermons and hymns must be accounted, even in the modern church, to be the most powerful agents of religious education, far in advance of the influence of religious publishing. And of those three elements, both liturgies and hymns must be classified as essentially conservative in character, hymns, because there is an obvious congregational preference for the familiar, and liturgies, because they are usually subject to close regulation by canon law. The situation is, therefore, that the laity and the ordinary clergy have a very powerful position when there break out, in the ordinary course of events, controversies as to Christian belief and practice. But it is essentially a conservative position, unless steps are taken to ensure the theological education of the laity and their incorporation in the corporate decisions of the church.

The signification of the reformation in this regard is precisely that it took the first steps towards the theological education of the laity by giving them the scriptures in the vernacular. Among the reformed ecclesiologies, congregationalism, the theory that each and every member of the church is equally responsible to God for the maintenance of the sole lordship of Christ over the church, represents the radical ecclesial expression of a fundamentally educational and social movement of democratic advancement. Whatever the future of democratisation in the church, the laity cannot be said to have readily risen to the role offered them in congregationalist theory. Nor, in Anglicanism, were they ever meant to do so. Here they are still lodged in an essentially conservative position, as an element checking the power of church leaders and theologians or, at the most, sharing (as in contemporary synodical government) in the process of decision-making on a carefully restricted basis.

Thus, for Anglicans, it still remains the case that the liturgy of the church creates the power base for the Christian community as a whole. This was so in the early church, and, with the gift of the scriptures in the vernacular, it becomes still more the case in Anglicanism. And the conclusion for contemporary Anglicanism must be that what is enforced in the liturgies of the church is the most powerful tool in the hands of ordinary clergy and the laity for resisting innovations which have no right to parity of esteem or equality of consideration when compared with the established traditions. Hence the decision-making process whereby liturgies are changed, as they must be with time, is the basic seat of authority in the Anglican church, and the basic exercise of that authority is the power to enforce the liturgy.

It has not, however, been explained how the participants in the processes of liturgical change are supposed to judge the numerous suggestions which are made to them. The answer to this question is difficult because neither of two obvious solutions are satisfactory. In the first place, it is not satisfactory to imagine that the modern church can reduplicate the arrangements of the primitive church. Liturgical scholarship includes, of course, the presentation of ancient liturgies for the consideration of the contemporary church. But liturgical judgement is not a matter of liturgical archaeology. Liturgies must change if the liturgical action is to remain the same. At the same time, personal preference, taste or pragmatic considerations without reference to any kind of precedent are basically inadequate. This is because the judgement as to what is essential to Christian profession has to be made on the basis of what is plainly to be heard in scripture.

We seem, then, to be in a cleft stick. On the one hand it is impossible to mould the liturgy of the church to make it reduplicate the apostolic community. On the other, it is impossible not to use the apostolic church as a criterion against the danger of purely adventitious deviations and distortions. Is it the case that one operates the celebrated method of selective blindness? That one appeals to the apostolic period when it suits one's convenience and ignores it when it does not? That you claim, for instance, that there is no doctrine of transubstantiation in the New Testament, but that the ordination of women is the will of the Holy Spirit?

The proper answer to this is, I believe, that a Christian must exercise his judgement, and that, I recognise, is scarcely an answer at all. But to put some flesh on the bones one might add that this judgement is like the judgement a novelist has to exercise when he or she brings a character to a particularly dramatic set of circumstances and must offer a plausible account of the character's response. It must be plausible in the sense that the character must act out of the resources which the novelist has created in earlier parts of the book and within the general limits of human psychology. In such a judgement there is both a predictable and a creative element, and the skill of a novelist lies in his ability to make the most of the fact that characters are interesting not because their actions can be predicted with certainty, but because the interaction of event and character creates geniune novelty.

This analogy is useful because so much of the resource which a Christian making decisions about liturgical change has at his disposal is in the form of narrative; what God has done in the history of Israel; what Jesus said and did, especially at the great climax of his life, when the interaction of event and character is observed with great closeness; and, also, what the history of the particular community, whose liturgy is taking new shape, has revealed of God's activity. It is out of these resources, and with a capacity to evoke the sense of continuity which is essential to the life of communities, that a judgement has to be made in the present circumstances which are necessarily unique. This church has to act in character; but what is in character may never have been done precisely like that before.

Hence the judgement which will be made will be necessarily controversial. Indeed in any given situation a multitude of different judgements will certainly be made, and conflict will result. And there will be no certainty that the decision made as a result of the conflict will be correct; thus before the next decision is made there must be careful observation of the consequences of the last one. This I believe to be the implication of the important notion of *process* introduced by the Lambeth Conference in 1948 into the consideration of the whole question of authority. While formally speaking, scripture, tradition and reason are norms of authority, the processes of decision-making in the Christian church are never completed. Decision-making is not, therefore, a matter of balancing one authority against another nor of holding authorities in tension, as Anglican writing has sometimes suggested. There is only one source of authority which is the freedom and love of the Triune God. In human life, in scripture, in the creeds, in the decisions of councils, in the liturgical order and canon law, in church leadership, there is only the discovery of authority, not its embodiment.

A remark must be made, finally, about the interpretation of 'oversight' (*episcope*) in Anglicanism. The Western Reformed Catholicism which typifies the Anglican communion has set great store by continuity, and of this the institution of episcopacy is the symbol. But Anglicanism is unable to offer a consistent theory of its own episcopacy unless it is willing to urge that in every place where there is an Anglican bishop, that bishop and not the Roman Catholic or Orthodox bishop is the true symbol of unity. Since the Anglican church has never claimed that in it alone is there to be found the fulness of the church, it follows that the theological interpretation of *its* episcopate is necessarily the interpretation of a partial and broken symbol of the continuity of faith. Too much Anglican writing about bishops is about the episcopacy of a church which does not exist. If one takes merely the first sentence of the section in the 1968 Lambeth Conference report on the nature of the episcopate one can see this problem. 'The bishop', it says, 'is called to lead the Church in the fulfilment of Christ's universal commission' (p. 108) The question is, what bishop and what church? Can it really be said of the Anglican communion that it 'possesses' the episcopate? In most parts of the world there is more than one bishop. If Anglicans are not saying that there is only one true bishop, and he the Anglican bishop, 'the bishop' who is the subject of this sentence and the whole of the section does not exist. And at the very least one imagines it would be helpful to today's bishops in the Anglican communion to discover what their vocation is in a broken church, and what its relation is to the true church. No Anglican should really be satisfied with any statement of the authority of oversight, which does not relate to the reality of the divided expression of church leadership.[2] For this reason I believe it is a matter of considerable wisdom that the present Anglican episcopate is unencumbered with any sharply defined theological theory. How the office of oversight is carried out meanwhile must be developed out of, and in conjunction with, a general understanding of the ministry of all Christian people.

My conclusion then is as follows: the dispersal of authority in Anglicanism is rooted in the conviction that Christians to whom the scriptures are read in their own language are able to judge of the essentials of the faith. Because it is a liturgical provision that the scriptures should be heard, and because the scriptures are contextualized in worship which seeks at once to evoke the fundamentals and induct the worshipper into the heart of Christian experience, decisions made about worship are crucial to the integrity of the faith. And decisions are unavoidable because liturgical arrangements must change. Because the decisions involved in change rest upon judgements, which are necessarly controversial, it is essential to the health of the church that it learn how to conduct controversy constructively and openly. Authority is not embodied, it is dispersed; and the reaching of authoritative decisions is a continuous process involving all the participators. In the context of this process Anglicans will want to place the role of leadership and oversight, with prime loyalty to their own leaders, but also with reference to the bishops and leaders of other denominations. In a broken church the episcopate which is the symbol of the continuity and integrity of the faith does not reside in any one person. Anglicans are, by the very terms of their own self-understanding, committed to labour for the restoration of that unity, and to offer the whole of the life and witness of their own communion in the service of the larger body of Christ's church which has existed from the dawn of humanity and will be consummated in the life and joy of the united worship of God in heaven.

FOOTNOTES

1. Report on the Book of Common Prayer, Part II, p. 80.
2. Cf. the passage in O.C. Quick, *The Christian Sacraments* (London, 1927), where, discussing the question whether all orders are not defective, he states: 'When the communion of the whole Church is divided, the representation of the whole Church in each congregation for these purposes [i.e. ordination] is no longer a reality; the will of Christ is hindered; and something essential to the very thing signified in ordination is no longer present', p. 145.

PATTERNS IN THEOLOGY

by Paul Wignall

SOME remarks earlier in the book indicate that, for modern theological study, the idea of a pattern in theology is far from self-explanatory. There are no grounds on which Anglicans (or anyone else) can be allowed to make passing references to patterns as though everyone could be expected to understand what was being said. On the contrary, the concept of a pattern, and its proper use in theology, are subjects of considerable complexity. A pattern in theology, like a pattern formulated in any other intellectual discipline, is an attempt to express clearly the result of sustained analytic endeavour. Far from allowing the theologian to dispense with thorough analysis — and in particular analysis of his methodological presuppositions — the concept of pattern requires a close examination of certain conceptual intricacies. Such examination is far from apparent in much contemporary theology.

What is offered here as a postscript to the discussion of Anglican theological method, can obviously be no more than an outline of what might be involved in taking seriously the concept 'pattern in theology'. At least I hope to show that a 'theological pattern' depends upon a wider context, and a larger set of elements, than is often allowed.

Professor Maurice Wiles, in his Hulsean Lectures on *The Remaking of Christian Doctrine* writes, in his 'Final Reflections':

> 'The pattern of belief that I have been trying to develop is belief in God upon whom the world depends for its very existence, a God who cares about human suffering, who has a purpose for the world which men can come in part at least to know, and who elicits from man a mature response to faith and love in which sin can begin to be overcome and the goals of human life begin to be realised.'[1]

This concise expression of a 'pattern of belief' may serve as a starting point for our discussion of patterns in theology.

Professor Wiles is, as it were, concerned to find an 'open space' in which the proper subject-matter of theology can be accurately expressed. Much of the *Remaking* is concerned with the delimitation of such a space. But an 'open space' is not an empty space. It is not the case that a theologian is presented with a *tabula rasa* (faith in God), upon which he can proceed to draw his pattern. On the contrary, the subject-matter of theology consists in a welter of complex and often conflicting ideas, actions and emotional states presented both by the tradition and by the contemporary world. It is to this complexity that the theologian addresses himself, and within which he professes to discern an order.

Wiles' 'pattern of belief' is, then, a theological proposal (which means both that it refers to God, and also stands in a particular intellectual discipline) about the way in which the world is ordered. In making this proposal he, as any other theologian, must select elements out of the infinitely complex world and suggest that they interpenetrate in such a way as to illuminate and organise all other elements. In trying to unravel the way in which Wiles arrives at his proposal, we may be able to discern certain fundamental features of theological pattern-making.

Professor Wiles carves out his open space by applying, as a critical tool, his understanding of the nature of God. Or, to change the metaphor and add another dimension, his understanding of the mode of God's presence in the world sets out the boundaries of acceptable theological discourse. Underlying the 'pattern of belief' is Wiles affirmation that

> 'Talk of God's activity. . . refrains from claiming any effective causation on the part of God in relation to particular occurrences. . .'[2]

God is to the world as a non-interfering Creator. A Creator who indeed 'cares', and who 'has a purpose for the world', but who does not express that purposive concern in ways that would traditionally be called 'acts of God'. God works only with and through the laws of nature, not against them. It is this critical tool which constrains theological discourse to keep within certain limits, and it is this same tool which can be wielded to make that delimited area into an open space (a formal garden rather than a jumbled wilderness) by effectively chopping down such dogmatic trees as Incarnation which spoil the view, and throwing the dead wood over the boundary fence.

Wiles is led to make his particular open space by his concern to uphold the causal independence of the created world. His assertion that the world must be allowed to be itself reminiscent at times of one side of Austin Farrer's understanding of divine creativity — dominates not only his pattern-making but also the (logically) prior formulation of the critical tool of 'God's "action" in the world'. In Farrer's words, 'God made the world. . . make itself'[3] ; Wiles transforms this notion into an exclusion of divine activity from the world except in the general case of purposive concern.

The making of Professor Wiles' 'pattern of belief' (or rather, its *remaking*, for the historian of theology can quickly recognise its ancestors) has this logical structure. He begins by asserting the causal independence of the created world over against its Creator. This leads him to outline a view of theology which takes this creaturely independence seriously as a starting point. From this understanding of the world, and the aim of theology — which is seen as in line with non-theological intellectual disciplines — he begins to construct a theological pattern which will express that understanding of reality. First of all he must find a tool which will clear the ground of obstructive elements. For Wiles this tool is a honed-down version of the prior vision of the world's independence. Application of the principle that divine 'activity' is not specific to certain events, removes those elements which speak in such terms from consideration for pattern-making (including, in this case, the doctrine of the Incarnation), and brings into prominence other elements, which are then expressed as a coherent 'pattern of belief'.

In fact, two separate selections have taken place. First, obstructions to the clarification of the original vision have been removed — certain ways of thinking are shown to be outside the pale of discourse — and second, a selection is made from the remaining elements bringing into prominence only those reckoned to be especially illuminating of the subject-matter as a whole. For a pattern precisely does not include every element within the open space which has been delimited, nor indeed is every element which is alien to the pattern removed. A pattern is a particular organisation of selected ideas made in an attempt to show the subject-matter to be a whole. Wiles' conception of the unity of theology as an expression of the unity of reality leads him to set traditional views of the Incarnation outside the pale of theology, and also to reinterpret the meaning of the life of Jesus by reference to that pattern of belief which he has proposed.

This is in many ways an oversimplification of what is a subtly constructed, though hardly original, position, but it may serve as a pointer to some essential elements in pattern-making. Four elements can be drawn out: the idea of *wholeness*, the idea of *selection*, the idea of a *constraint*, and the idea of a *route-finding procedure*.

(1) A particular theological position — whether articulated by the professional theologian, or appropriated by other Christians — is an expression of a belief in the unity of all things in God. The theologian seeks to formulate — often in the rarified atmosphere of intellectual debate — a clear expression of his view of 'the way things hang together'. A theological position is a 'pattern of belief' which is also a 'pattern of ideas'. That is, the theologian attempts, by his pattern-making, to express his faith in God, and his understanding of God's way with the world. As an expression of the wholeness of the subject-matter of theology, a pattern of belief is something to be discovered by paying attention to the world, and by deep study of the patterns of belief of others. But, at the same time, this pattern of belief, as a pattern of ideas, expresses another sort of unity. Not only is the theologian concerned to express his vision of the coherence of the world, but he is also concerned to formulate a coherent position: to construct a pattern of ideas as immune as possible from the criticism of others. It is vital that these two sorts of coherence are not confused, for a coherent theological position can only be, at best, an approximation to the coherence of reality. A pattern of ideas can only be an illuminating approximation to 'the way things hang together'. When making a pattern a theologian is attempting to communicate a vision of wholeness.

(2) Because a theological pattern of ideas is an intellectual construct which seeks to express a logically prior understanding of what it means to believe in God, the theologian must *select* those aspects of his subject-matter which seem to him most adequately to illuminate the totality of his subject-matter, and which reveal the subject-matter as having a particular sort of wholeness. The notion of selection, of course, tends to have pejorative overtones: accusations of selectivity are often thought to be the most damning of all criticisms. Selection is indeed a dangerous procedure, but it is absolutely necessary. The complexity of the world is itself too chaotic to manifest

patterns; the order in the world, if such order there is, can only be revealed by a process of abstraction, of selection, and, to use Sir Herbert Butterfield's term, of 'abridgement'.[4] The danger lies in confusing the comparative simplicity of the abridgement with a supposed simplicity in the world. Selections and abridgements, in theology no less than in history, need constantly to be tested by reference back to the complexity of the world. The critic must always ask: does this particular pattern, selected as it is from such a welter of ideas, in fact illuminate the complexity, or does it oversimplify? Patterns must be tested by reference back to the totality from which they are drawn.

(3) A theologian's pattern is an attempt to provide the rules for the theological 'game'. In fact, in theology, it is not possible to state in advance what the rules of the game are with any degree of certainty. But the theologian is presented by the tradition of theological discourse, as well as by the conditions of cross-disciplinary debate, with certain constraints upon his pattern-making. For example, a theological position which took seriously only the so-called Johannine writings and sought to discover the pattern inherent in them ('the Johannine position'), would be constrained to interpret the life of Jesus in particular ways, and not in others. In such a case the 'Johannine position' (should such a thing exist) would act as the basic constraint upon all the patterning procedures which that theologian was involved in – the sort of wholeness sought, and the way in which selection was guided, for instance. The role of criticism in theology requires a close study of the constraints a theologian builds into his pattern-making: what he takes to be 'authority' for a particular proposal. Such 'authority' not only constrains the theologian in his pattern-making, it also acts as the principle of delimitation, setting up the boundary fence within which a theological pattern is to be made.

(4) A physics text-book defines a pattern as 'the smallest piece of the whole design which displays both the basic unit and its inter-relationship with other units.' It is always dangerous to transfer definitions from one discipline to another, but the connection between the concept of pattern in physics and in theology is, at this level of generality, helpful. A theological pattern is an orderly arrangement of certain key ideas made in an attempt to express the order inherent in the subject-matter from which the selection is made. The pattern not only

expresses an internal order but also seeks to point to the way in which ideas external to the pattern, but internal to the subject-matter, are ordered. Here again, an example may be helpful. In a fascinating study of Christology, L.S. Thornton sought to express the wholeness of reality by reference to an argued wholeness in the Church's scriptures, discerned in the dominance of a particular pattern of ideas.[5] Such a controlling image he found in Markan account of the events from Peter's confession of Jesus as Messiah, through to the Transfiguration. This pattern of events is interpreted by Thornton as expressive of the victory of God over chaos. A typological analysis of different parts of the Old and New Testaments is made to support the claim that Jesus himself is the organising principle of this pattern. The pattern of events leading up to the Trans-figuration is taken by Thornton to be 'the smallest piece of the whole design which displays both the basic unit (divine victory over chaos personified in Jesus) and its inter-relationship with other units.' To understand the Transfiguration narratives, says Thornton, is to have discovered how to find your way around in the complexities of theology.

It has been suggested that 'a theologian's pattern is an attempt to provide the rules for the theological game.' In what sense is theology a 'game'? In a study of the debate about 'New Testament theology', Robert Morgan writes:

> 'a chess player has a definite aim, and the strategy behind his moving pieces around the board is dictated by that. Similarly, in interpreting the whole tradition to reach a cogent theological position a theologian must so marshal the evidence of the tradition that an opponent has to admit the superiority of his position. [6]

In some ways, of course, the theological game is not like a chess game — above all, the rules of the game are not necessarily decided in advance in theology. But the theological game does resemble chess in use of tradition to provide strategies. Gambits in chess can be learnt by studying past games. But this is to side-step Morgan's point. For him, the tradition provides the pieces for the game rather than the rules and so the formulation of a theological position requires reflection upon the tradition. Like a chess-set, the theological tradition has an objective quality: the pieces are there and we must get on with the game. Sacrifices are possible in theology no less than in chess. In order to persuade an opponent of the coherence of a position, the theologian may have to ignore certain 'pieces' given by the tradition — selection takes place. Three points can be made about this. First, selection is not necessarily a bad thing — after all chess games are sometimes won after the sacrifice of a queen. The important thing is what is done with the pieces that *are* on the board. Second, sacrifices may prove to be fatal mistakes — the piece may turn out to be fundamental to the winning of *any* game (a queen can be sacrificed, a king cannot). And third, as Morgan points out:

> 'after every game of theological interpretation all the pieces of tradition come back onto the board. The set would be impaired if part of the tradition were destroyed. Theological criticism does not mutilate the tradition by annihilating what is thought to be unacceptable.'[7]

Because theology is an historical discipline no theologian can finally dispose of any element of the tradition; all that he can do is to try to show its inappropriateness to his particular attempt to express what theology is about. He may formulate his position by dismissing certain elements entirely from the field of debate but, because there are histories of theology he cannot expunge it totally from the potential apparatus of the theologians of succeeding generations. Old battles are fought anew with a regularity which becomes tedious only when combatants fail to recognise that they are old battles.

It is a fundamental constraint upon theological pattern-making that it is a *game* that is being played in the sense that 'the pieces go back onto the board for others to use'. The sheer objectivity of the data of theology is a fundamental feature of pattern-making.

The theological tradition has been constantly involved in a reappraisal of the rules of its game, and of the theoretical open space available for the patterning. Frequently this reappraisal is formulated in terms of the question, how is scripture to be used?

'Scripture' is, of course, an ecclesiastical term. To call a book, or collection of books, 'scripture' is to say that here is something which a religious community sees as a key expression of its belief in the way in which the world is shown to have an order. But scripture has no unmediated presence in the community, precisely because it is a 'holy book', whose primary use is in worship. The centrality of scripture to the worshipping life of a community brings into focus the uses of scripture for other aspects of its life — in ethics, for instance, or even in learning to read and write. Above all, the church's use of the bible as scripture decisively influences the theologian's understanding of his subject-matter. In a recent contribution to hermeneutics, Professor D.H. Kelsey has argued that the dominant criterion for a theologian's understanding of scripture is to be found in

> 'the concrete details of the common life of the Christian community as the theologian experiences it by participating in it'.[8]

We can move beyond Kelsey's immediate concern and suggest that the most important aspect of 'the common life of the Christian community' is its gathering for worship, for it is precisely at this point that the community finds itself in that theoretical open space in which patterns of belief can be worked out, and in which faith can grow.

But the worship of the church is itself an historical development. In this it mirrors (precisely) the constant reappraisal of the church's understanding of scripture. It is in this sense that the context of pattern-making is much wider than is often recognised. The theologian cannot simply be concerned with his own academic tradition, or with the Bible as a series of historical documents (although he needs a detailed working knowledge of both), for, as his pattern of ideas is also a pattern of belief, he must recognise that the expression of a community's faith in its worship actually mediates both his attitude to his tradition, and his understanding of the Bible. This does not mean that the theologian cannot criticise the worship and belief of the church of which he is a part, but it does mean that the objectivity of the data of theology is brought home to him every time he goes to his parish church or his college chapel. For Anglicans the Book of Common Prayer and its various revisions provides an open space in which faith can grow and patterns can be made; and the theologian needs to give good reasons for redefining the boundaries of that space. He must give good reasons precisely because liturgy is a conservative source in that it forces the theologian to recognise that he is playing the game with pieces that are presented to him. So long as a particular form of worship remains unchanged (so long as it retains a particular set of pieces and a particular board) he must give very good reasons for suggesting that a new way of playing the game be adopted, with less or more pieces.

Theological method, then, has an historical element. Just as chess players study the games of past Grand Masters and learn gambits which they can apply for themselves, so theologians study the theological tradition to see how techniques have been forged and used in the past. The pieces stay the same and many strategies are unchanged, but the games are ever new. Theological positions remain attempts to communicate a vision — a belief — with the greatest clarity. The vision is *my* vision, although it is my vision of. . .; my construction is *mine*; the notes of my observations are *my* notes of *my* observations, even though my observatory is the worshipping life of the church of which I am a part. Other people's patterns have a role to play in the formulation of my pattern, in the communication of my understanding of the way things are — they may even mould my pattern entirely. But, in the end, the attempt to discover is *my* voyage, and the pattern made on the voyage is an account of my travels for the assistance of other travellers. Only if that account is made clearly and responsibly can it begin to illuminate, or even perhaps point towards, the infinitely complex reality of God, who is the object of our journey and the path of our travelling.

FOOTNOTES

1. M. F. Wiles, *The Remaking of Christian Doctrine,* (London, 1974) pp. 116f.
2. *Remaking,* p. 38.
3. A. Farrer, *A Celebration of Faith,* (London, 1970), p. 73.
4. Selectivity in historical analysis is examined in a penetrating manner in Butterfield's *The Whig Interpretation of History.*
5. L. S. Thornton, *The Form of a Servant,* (Westminster, 1950 & 1952).
6. R. C. Morgan, *The Nature of New Testament Theology,* (London, 1973), pp. 43f.
7. Morgan, op. cit., p. 44.
8. D. H. Kelsey, *The Uses of Scripture in Recent Theology,* (London, 1975), p. 193.

Appendix

1. Letter from the Reverend Professor H. E. Root, to *The Times* dated May 29, and published on June 1, 1977.

Sir, Dr. Peacocke's letter (May 28) in reply to that of the Roman Catholic Bishop of East Anglia is important because of its positive affirmations as well as its seeming innocence of what the Bishop was talking about. I write as an Anglican member of the Anglican/Roman Catholic International Commission.

Despite the letters of Dr. Peacocke and, earlier, of Canon Drury (May 18), the main point has been missed. Within the Commission (as well as outside it) there has been no problem about the legitimacy of diversity (or 'comprehensiveness') in matters of theological interpretation. Our Agreed Statements speak for themselves in this matter. No member of the Commission has sought to find a final, inflexible formula of theological interpretation. On neither side is there a desire to return to a position of 'non-historical orthodoxy'. As our Statements make quite clear, theological formulations, both ancient and modern, must always be interpreted in contemporary terms. This is not an easy exercise, but it is one which we commonly accept as necessary in the quest for truth and the process of restoring of unity between Rome and Canterbury.

There are, however, limits to diversity. There can be no real unity in faith unless we are agreed on what can properly be called 'fundamentals'. Anglicans, not surprisingly, feel that some (in particular, some relatively modern) Roman Catholic definitions and formulations are not self-evidentally fundamental to Christian faith, however much we may understand and appreciate them in their historical context. On the other side, Roman Catholics have serious and genuine questions about whether Anglicans hold to any 'fundamentals' at all.

In contrast to some of the views of your correspondents, my notion is that the division is not between the two Churches, but that it cuts across 'denominational' loyalties. Some Roman Catholic and some Anglican writers seem, in varying ways, to erode the distinction between fundamentals of faith and those theological interpretations which may change from age to age.

Your Anglican correspondents seem to me right to stress the importance of comprehensiveness. Your Roman Catholic correspondents are no less right in questioning where comprehensiveness ends and adherence to fundamentals begins. My own experience leads me to believe that, on both sides, there is common faith. We are agreed upon 'the Nicene faith', that Christ was the incarnate Word of God. Much issues from this. But this is the point from which we begin. For theologians these terms require constant investigation and interpretation. But theologians are secondary people.

Their agreements and disagreements are important for but not essential to the life of the Christian Church. If, however, it were true that many Anglican or Roman Catholic Christians could not accept this fundamental affirmation (or were hesitant about it) we should have to ask whether there is any point in continuing to search for unity. Christian faith (whether in Anglican or Roman Catholic expression) would cease to be Christian.

We may have unresolved questions about what follows from an acceptance of our fundamental faith. That is not surprising after 400 years of separation. But we can scarcely dare to work, or hope to move further, unless we are convinced that upon this fundamental rock we are already agreed.

Yours faithfully,
H. E. ROOT,
Department of Theology and Religion,
The University, Southampton.

2. An Appended note 'On Assent', printed at the end of a chapter 'On the Sources and Authority of Christian Doctrine', in *Doctrine in the Church of England*, The Report of the Commission on Christian Doctrine Appointed by the Archbishops of Canterbury and York in 1922 (London, 1938), pp. 38–9.

On Assent

With a view to the avoidance of misunderstanding of what is said in the above Note, and elsewhere in this Report, the Commission desires to place on record the following resolutions:

1. The Christian Church exists on the basis of the Gospel which has been entrusted to it.

2. General acceptance, implicit if not explicit, of the authoritative formularies, doctrinal and liturgical, by which the meaning of the Gospel has been defined, safeguarded, or expressed, may reasonably be expected from members of the Church.

3. Assent to formularies and the use of liturgical language in public worship should be understood as signifying such general acceptance without implying detailed assent to every phrase or proposition thus employed.

4. Subject to the above, a member of the Church should not be held to be involved in dishonesty merely on the ground that, in spite of some divergence from the tradition of the Church, he has assented to formularies or makes use of the Church's liturgical language in public worship.

The above considerations apply to the authorised teachers as well as to all other members of the Church; but the position of the authorised teacher is distinctive, and the Church has a right to satisfy itself that those who teach in its name adequately represent and express its mind.

5. No individual can claim to receive the teacher's commission as a right, and the commission itself involves the obligation not to teach, as the doctrine of the Church, doctrine which is not in accordance with the Church's mind.

6. If any authorised teacher puts forward personal opinions which

diverge (within the limits indicated above) from the traditional teaching of the Church, he should be careful to distinguish between such opinions and the normal teaching which he gives in the Church's name; and so far as possible such divergences should be so put forward as to avoid offending consciences.

7. In respect of the exercise of discipline within such limits as the above resolutions recognise, great regard should be paid to the need for securing a free consensus, as distinct from an enforced uniformity.

N.B — Some members of the Commission while not dissenting from these resolutions, are of opinion that No. 6 gives by implication too wide a latitude, and would press more strongly the obligation resting upon all who hold office in the Church to believe and to teach the traditional doctrine of the Church.

3. A section entitled 'The Meaning and Unity of the Anglican Communion' from a Committee of Bishops reporting on 'The Anglican Communion', printed in *The Lambeth Conference 1948* (London, 1948), Part II, pp. 84-86.

The world is in grievous disorder and needs to be restored to the order which God wills. A perplexed generation is in search of an authority to which to give its allegiance, and easily submits to the appeal of authoritarian systems whether religious or secular in character.

The question is asked, 'Is Anglicanism based on a sufficiently coherent form of authority to form the nucleus of a world-wide fellowship of Churches, or does its comprehensiveness conceal internal divisions which may cause its disruption?'

Former Lambeth Conferences have wisely rejected proposals for a formal primacy of Canterbury, for an Appellate Tribunal and for giving the Conference the status of a legislative synod. The Lambeth Conference remains advisory, and its continuation committee consultative.

These decisions have led to a repudiation of centralized government, and a refusal of a legal basis of union.

The positive nature of the authority which binds the Anglican Communion together is therefore seen to be moral and spiritual, resting on the truth of the Gospel, and on a charity which is patient and willing to defer to the common mind.

Authority, as inherited by the Anglican Communion from the undivided Church of the early centuries of the Christian era, is single in that it is derived from a single Divine source, and reflects within itself the richness and historicity of the divine Revelation, the authority of the eternal Father, the incarnate Son, and the life-giving Spirit. It is distributed among Scripture, Tradition, Creeds, the Ministry of the Word and Sacraments, the witness of saints, and the *consensus fidelium,* which is the continuing experience of the Holy Spirit through His faithful people in the Church. It is thus a dispersed rather than a centralized authority having many elements which combine, interact with, and check each other; these elements together contributing by a process of mutual support, mutual checking, and redressing of errors or exaggerations to the many-sided fullness of the authority which Christ has committed to His Church. Where this authority of Christ is to be found mediated not in one mode but in several we recognize in this multiplicity God's loving provision against the temptations to tyranny and the dangers of unchecked power.

This authority possesses a suppleness and elasticity in that the emphasis of one element over the others may and does change with the changing conditions of the Church. The variety of the contributing factors gives to it a quality of richness which encourages and releases initiative, trains in fellowship, and evokes a free and willing obedience.

It may be said that authority of this kind is much harder to understand and obey than authority of a more imperious character. This is true and we glory in the appeal which it makes to faith. Translated into personal terms it is simple and intelligible. God who is our ultimate personal authority demands of all His creatures entire and unconditional obedience. As in human families the father is the mediator of this divine authority, so in the family of the Church is the bishop, the Father-in-God, wielding his authority by virtue of his divine commission and in synodical association with his clergy and laity, and exercising it in humble submission, as himself under authority.

The elements in authority are, moreover, in organic relation to each other. Just as the discipline of the scientific method proceeds from the collection of data to the ordering of these data in formulæ, the publishing of results obtained, and their verification by experience, so Catholic Christianity presents us with an organic process of life and thought in which religious experience has been, and is, described, intellectually ordered, mediated, and verified.

This experience is *described* in Scripture, which is authoritative because it is the unique and classical record of the revelation of God in His relation to and dealings with man. While Scripture therefore remains the ultimate standard of faith, it should be continually interpreted in the context of the Church's life.

It is *defined* in Creeds and in continuous theological study.

It is *mediated* in the ministry of the Word and Sacraments, by persons who are called and commissioned by God through the Church to represent both the transcendent and immanent elements in Christ's authority.

It is *verified* in the witness of saints and in the *consensus fidelium*. The Christ-like life carries its own authority, and the authority of doctrinal formulations, by General Councils or otherwise, rests at least in part on their acceptance by the whole body of the faithful, though the weight of this *consensus* 'does not depend on mere numbers or on the extension of a belief at any one time, but on continuance through the ages, and the extent to which the *consensus* is genuinely free.'

This essentially Anglican authority is reflected in our adherence to episcopacy as the source and centre of our order, and the Book of Common Prayer as the standard of our worship. Liturgy, in the sense of the offering and ordering of the public worship of God, is the crucible in which these elements of authority are fused and unified in the fellowship and power of the Holy Spirit. It is the Living and Ascended Christ present in the worshipping congregation who is the meaning and unity of the whole Church. He presents it to the Father, and sends it out on its mission.

We therefore urge the whole Conference to call upon every member of the Anglican Communion to examine himself in respect of his obligation to public worship.

We recognize that our fellow-Churchmen in some parts of the world do not always express themselves in worship according to Western patterns, and that they must have generous liberty of experiment in liturgy; and we therefore reaffirm Resolutions 36 and 37 of the Conference of 1920.

But we appeal to those who are responsible for the ordering and conduct of public worship to remember how bewildered the laity are by differences of use, and with what earnest care and charity they should be helped to take their full share in liturgical worship.

We consider that the time has come to examine those 'features in the Book fo Common Prayer which are essential to the safeguarding of the unity of the Anglican Communion' (Resolution 37, 1920) and the Recommendations of Committee IV of 1920.

INDEX

INDEX